The Museum Curator's Guide

The Museum Curator's Guide

Understanding, Managing and Presenting Objects

Nicola Pickering

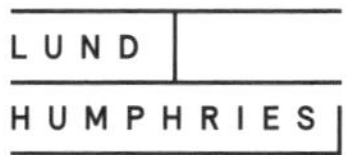

For S.P.P. and M.B.R.P.

First published in 2020 by Lund Humphries

Lund Humphries
Office 3, Book House
261A City Road
London EC1V 1JX
UK

www.lundhumphries.com

ISBN (paperback): 978-1-84822-324-0
ISBN (PDF): 978-1-84822-413-1
ISBN (ePub): 978-1-84822-414-8
ISBN (Mobi): 978-1-84822-415-5

A Cataloguing-in-Publication record for this book is available from the British Library.

Printed in the United Kingdom

Contents

Preface

A museum curator is generally responsible for a collection of objects, ensuring that they are suitably preserved for the future, understood and appreciated, and displayed and interpreted for the public in some way. The role of curator encompasses a variety of duties and can involve a certain degree of complexity. The work a curator undertakes must support the mission of a museum to educate and entertain the public through the care, arrangement, study and display of objects. A curator will take responsibility for the development of a collection and direct the collecting of new objects. They must also manage these collections and associated information in accordance with recognised sector standards. Curators today continue to carry out scholarly research and produce outputs that will communicate information and understanding about historic objects, past lives and culture to a variety of audiences. The role of a curator, and the duties they may be expected to perform, can vary widely between different organisations.

This publication is intended as a useful, practical guide, exploring the work of a museum curator as described above. It considers why museums exist, how objects are treated and displayed in museums, and the role of the curator, their interactions with, and work to care for, objects. This book draws together these subjects and presents them succinctly: it is a much-needed reference work, combining information on all the major duties and activities of the museum curator in one volume.

While many major aspects of work of the curator in museums today have been addressed, along with elements of museology, inevitably it has not been possible to explore every conceivable angle in this short guide. Further information and guidance on the subjects covered in the publication can be found in the sources named in the endnotes for each chapter. Similarly, it would have been impossible to examine the full range of subjects and discussions pertaining to the field of museology within the limits of the publication: a selection of the scholarship relating to some of the major museological debates is also included in the endnotes of this volume as suggestions for further reading.

This book will be of interest to emerging professionals working in the museums sector, students of museum studies and heritage management, as well as private collectors and individuals seeking guidance in caring for and displaying historic objects. As a result, the content of this guide has been deliberately presented in an accessible manner, avoiding overcomplicated styles of expression and unnecessarily complex terms and vocabulary.

As a result of the author's personal experience and professional expertise, the content of the volume refers most particularly to museums within the UK. The ideas and guidance presented, however, can be applied to the activity of museums across the world. The topics examined in this publication have been considered using a predominantly theoretical approach. In order to provide as full an overview of the many aspects of a museum curator's work as possible, a large number of subjects are examined in this publication. As a result, within the context of the nature of this book, it has not been possible to produce extensive case studies to illustrate all topics.

Acknowledgements

I am extremely grateful to Professor Jean Michael Massing and Michael Stradling for their comments on the draft of this publication. I would also like to acknowledge the generous support of my publisher at Lund Humphries, Lucy Clark, for this, my first book.

Introduction

What are museum curators, and what do they do?

The term curator, as applied to the museum, grew from the word's origins in caring for and having guardianship of something.[1] A curator generally cares for a museum's collection, assisting the organisation to fulfil its mission to educate and entertain the public through the care, arrangement, study and display of objects. In the 21st century, visitors to museums are often seeking content, and it is usually the curator's responsibility to provide the information for this content and to establish the most suitable methods of presenting it.[2] As the dominance of the scholar-curator has waned in modern museums, duties such as collections management, conservation, enabling public access and facilitating learning have increasingly become part of the core work of curatorial staff.[3] The functions and responsibilities of many specialist museological roles also involve a range of administrative and management duties: many curators at all stages of their careers manage data, schedules, projects, budgets and staff.

This book examines the major aspects of the work of a curator, from collecting objects and collections management to carrying out research and producing exhibitions. By way of an introduction, the main functions and duties of a museum curator are outlined below:

COLLECTING AND DEVELOPMENT (CHAPTER 2)

A curator will engage in the act of collecting new objects for the museum and this will require an appropriate level of subject-specialist knowledge. Part of a curator's role will be to consider the strategic direction of all activity relating to collecting of objects in the museum (expressed in the museum's Collections Development Policy).

COLLECTIONS AND INFORMATION MANAGEMENT (CHAPTERS 3 AND 4)

In the last 50 years, countries all over the world have worked to devise and implement professional standards in collections management and care, in attempts to standardise previously haphazard and inconsistent approaches. The curator must find ways to apply these statements, guidelines and/or requirements in practice to whichever museum collection they are responsible for.

COLLECTIONS CARE (CHAPTER 5)

Whether on display or in store, museum objects need to be adequately cared for, and a curator needs to be keenly aware of the main ways through which to achieve this, working closely with conservators. A curator's subject-specific knowledge about the museum's collections will enable them to make informed decisions.

CREATING DISPLAYS AND CONTENT (CHAPTERS 6 AND 7)

A curator is likely to be one of the primary members of staff responsible for producing permanent and temporary displays or exhibitions. They may be involved to varying degrees, according to the size and nature of an organisation. In general, curators are involved in the selection of themes and objects, the research of content and composition of interpretation and supporting materials.

COMMUNICATION (CHAPTERS 6 AND 7)

Curators are expected to communicate information and engage in storytelling relating to the museum's collections to a wide range of users. Frequently, curators must summarise complex ideas and communicate them in an appropriate and clear manner. Curators are expected to produce written content for all kinds of reasons and at all levels, so a facility for language is an advantage in this regard (for example, in reports, policies, proposals, academic texts, debates, comment pieces, interpretation, press releases, website content).

ACCESS (CHAPTER 8)

Part of a curator's role is to enable access to collection objects, and to the services the museum offers. Many issues relating to collections care and security must be carefully considered in order to balance the protection of objects with the wish to provide access. Curators should seek to ensure collection objects are actively used, accessible and promoted to the public: this might be through the use of objects in displays, learning and other public events, collections websites, accessible museum stores, loans to other organisations and touring exhibitions.

LEARNING (CHAPTER 8)

In the modern museum, all curators must also be educators: they must explain and present information and ideas to a range of audiences in a variety of formats, using a broad range of methods. The social engagement aspect of working with collections is an increasingly important part of curatorial work.

RESEARCH (CHAPTER 9)

Museum collections are only as valuable as the documented knowledge about them, and carrying out original, in-depth research that can expand this knowledge will strengthen all museum activities. There is a long tradition of scholarly research connected to museum collections, yet the place of this research in museums has been rigorously scrutinised in recent years. The attitude of different institutions to the role and value of research is increasingly divergent and, in some museums, research will be considered as less of a priority. It is equally possible that sufficient time may not be available for curatorial staff to carry out this function, which may be overshadowed by the large volume of work necessary in the areas of collections management and care.

MANAGEMENT RESPONSIBILITY

Many curators also undertake work in areas such as strategic leadership, project management and people management. All museums will have a staff structure, and as a curator becomes more senior, they will be expected to take on responsibility for the coordination and management of the output of varying sizes of teams.[4]

FUNDRAISING, MARKETING AND COMMERCIAL ACTIVITY

The basic functions of a museum in collecting and preserving objects, and providing opportunities for the public to access and interact with those objects, can only be maintained with enough money to pay staff and maintain premises. Many museums are not awarded enough public funding to achieve this and must pursue other avenues of income generation (for example, short-term discrete grants, public fundraising, private sponsorship, venue hire, retail and catering). A curator may be involved in all these activities in varying degrees.

SPECIALISATION

While some curators care for collections containing a diverse range of objects, covering broad time periods, geographical areas and connected subject areas, many curators retain a subject specialism and are experts in the care and display of particular types of object. Indeed, certain collections must be cared for by curators who have specialist knowledge and experience (for example, natural history collections). It is common for large museums to appoint curators with responsibility for just one part of the collections (for example, paintings, sculpture, textiles, archaeology).

Depending on the size and nature of an organisation, curatorial departments may be made up of several different staff specialities, including, for example, registrars, collections managers, interpretation managers, exhibition coordinators, cataloguers, archivists, librarians, conservators and curators. This may mean that a curator is expected to focus more on duties such as research and communication, as work relating to collections management and care is undertaken by those in other specialist roles.[5] A small museum may not be able to appoint such a range of staff and one curator may be expected to carry out the majority of these functions.

PART ONE

MUSEUMS AND COLLECTIONS

1

What are museums?

ICOM, the International Council of Museums, was formed in 1946 as an international non-governmental organisation. It maintains formal relations with UNESCO (the United Nations Educational, Scientific and Cultural Organization, a specialised agency of the United Nations), and has a consultative status with the United Nations' Economic and Social Council.[1] ICOM supports a network of museum professionals all around the world and is 'committed to the conservation, continuation and communication to society of the world's natural and cultural heritage, present and future, tangible and intangible.'[2] When thinking about what a museum is, we might begin with ICOM's current definition:

> A museum is a non-profit, permanent institution in the service of society and its development, open to the public, which acquires, conserves, researches, communicates and exhibits the tangible and intangible heritage of humanity and its environment for the purposes of education, study and enjoyment.[3]

This definition contains a number of points that are worth further exploration. First, that according to ICOM, a museum is an 'institution', thus an organisation that is somehow formally governed. Furthermore, that it should be a 'non-profit' organisation, so one that is not actively attempting to make a profit and is instead investing any extra income back into the work of the organisation (in contrast to a theme park or popular entertainment venue). Being 'open to the public' seems today to be an obvious requirement of a museum (though it was not always so), and that museums should 'acquire' and 'conserve' heritage also seems an important requisite: this implies that a museum is an organisation that acquires objects because they will assist in fulfilling its purpose, and it will retain and maintain them.[4] Furthermore, being able to 'communicate and exhibit' the heritage of both 'humanity and its environment' is naturally equally essential: such a phrase asserts that a museum should allow visitors to see the objects it holds, and that they should be interpreted. Finally, the inclusion of a reference to both 'tangible and intangible' heritage is revealing, reflecting a change in our attitudes towards the nature of heritage, and recognising that it can be both physical (for example, objects and buildings) or non-physical (for example, folk law, dance, oral traditions, memories).

Several things about this ICOM definition may be called into question. For example, it is suggested that museums should be 'permanent', and that they ought to have longevity and the ability to develop over time. This criterion thus excludes the idea of 'pop-up' museums or one-off ephemeral endeavours. The inclusion of the phrase 'in the service of society and its development' is rather utopian, but we might ask what exactly a society is, and how such a society ought to develop. Finally, there are elements of the definition which invite further consideration: are 'research' and 'education' essential parts of a museum's work, and what does it mean to 'study' humans and their environment? Furthermore, we might dwell on the idea of 'enjoyment' within museums: must our experiences in museum spaces necessarily be enjoyable? These questions are ones that are commonly debated in the museums sector and will be addressed in subsequent chapters of this book.[5]

The origins of museums

In order to explore what museums are today, what they do, and what they are good for, it is necessary to explore the origins of this institution in Europe. The collecting of objects that might have religious, magical, economic, aesthetic or historical value, or that might simply be curiosities, has been carried out all over the world by individuals and groups for thousands of years.[6] The idea that collections of objects should be preserved and displayed to a public audience is a fundamental difference between some of the earliest museums and collections and museums of today.

Historians often wish to identify the first museum: a collection of objects preserved and on show to a public audience.[7] Some attention in this regard has been given to the Ennigaldi-Nanna museum in Ur (present day Iraq): in 1925 archaeologist Leonard Woolley discovered the oldest known curated collection of objects while excavating a Babylonian palace dating to *c.*530 BCE.[8] These came from many different places and times, and were arranged and labelled as if they were intended to be viewed and studied.[9] The curator of this 'museum' is thought to have been Princess Ennigaldi, the daughter of King Nabonidus, the last king of the Neo-Babylonian Empire.[10] Yet it is difficult to ascertain how open this collection was to public audiences, being located within a palace complex.

Scholarship and the 'museion' in the classical world

The term 'museion', as used in the classical world (c.8th century BCE to 5th or 6th century CE in Europe), is said to be the source of the modern usage of the word 'museum'.[11] In the classical Greek world a *museion*, or *mouseion*, was the name for a temple to (or under the protection of), the nine muses, ancient Greek goddesses, personifications of knowledge and the arts and daughters of Zeus. The Musaeum or Mouseion at Alexandria, Egypt, was one of the most famous examples, established in 280 BCE by Ptolemy I Soter (*c.*367–c.283 BCE).[12] Its origins owed much to the Lyceum founded by Aristotle in ancient Athens in the mid-340s BCE, a place in which a community of scholars and students could meet for systematic study, much like modern-day universities. It was at the Lyceum that the association of a 'museum' with collecting and studying objects began; here, Aristotle collected, examined, recorded and classified botanical material. Yet, while there may have been a library of sorts at the Lyceum and in the Mouseion at Alexandria, objects such as those we find in museums today were generally not housed here.

There were, however, other collections of objects in the classical Greek world: sometimes offerings in temples or treasuries that were open to the public included paintings, statues, exotic items and natural curiosities.[13] The Greek ruler of Pergamon, Attalus I Soter (241–197 BCE) collected paintings and statues from the lands he conquered and installed them in outdoor spaces or indoor galleries.[14] Similar use of statuary was evident in ancient Rome between 200 and 60 BCE: as the Roman empire expanded, Greek statuary was used to adorn the increasing number of new buildings and monuments, an advert for the power and reach of the state.[15]

Medieval Europe, the Renaissance and private collections

During the medieval period in Europe (broadly the 5th to the 15th centuries CE) the ownership of collections of culturally important, artistic, curious or valuable objects was generally restricted to those who were wealthy and powerful. Personal collections of art and sculpture, created by monarchs, church leaders or aristocrats, were intended to impress and also to represent piety, and they could also be of economic importance. Reflecting this activity, by the 1500s, two new words entered the Italian language: the *galleria* (a long, grand room with paintings and sculptures, lit from one side), and the *gabinetto* (a square-shaped room featuring natural history specimens, coins and curiosities). In Germany, the words *Kammer* or *Kabinett* began to be used for specially designated and secure rooms (specifically a *Kunstkammer* for art, *Schatzkammer* for high value religious or artistic 'treasures' and *Rustkammer* for collections of armour). In English, the word gallery now referred to a place where paintings and sculpture were shown. Yet these were overwhelmingly private spaces, accessed only by other privileged individuals or for private entertainment for a select audience.

The revival of classical learning and values which followed the medieval period was a significant time for the development of the private collection in Europe. The Renaissance period (broadly 1450 to 1700 CE) was an age of curiosity, exploration and invention, and travel and commercial activity flourished. Such an atmosphere, with a greater access to objects and specimens, encouraged wealthy and scholarly individuals to assemble collections of man-made objects such as coins, medals, paintings and statuary of intellectual, artistic or monetary importance (*artificialia*) alongside natural specimens or curiosities (*naturalia*).[16] The accepted practice was to arrange and classify the objects in cabinets or cases, in designated spaces in the residence or workplace of the collector ('cabinets of curiosity' or '*Wunderkammer*'). Here, special guests and fellow collectors could be entertained, the collections exhibiting the owner's power, refinement and education.[17] A select few of these collections could be viewed by privileged members of the public, though usually on a restricted basis and requiring special permission.

Enlightenment thought and the museum

The Enlightenment period (broadly the late 17th and early 18th centuries) was a very important moment for the development of museums in Europe and saw the foundation of organisations that most closely resemble museums today. During this period of Enlightenment philosophy, world exploration and developing industrialisation, people once again attempted to make sense of the world through the collection and scientific categorisation of objects, especially those they felt were exotic, unusual or curious. Importantly, by the end of the 17th century several new institutions referred to as 'museums' had been founded in Europe, ones tasked with enabling access to cultural patrimony for the general public.

Britain's oldest museum is often considered as the Royal Armouries in the Tower of London: from 1592, elite members of the public could apply for permission to view the collections, and in 1660, a wider public could pay to see certain staged displays. The first municipally owned public collection in the world is thought to be the Amerbach Cabinet of Basel, Switzerland: in 1661, the city purchased the collection of the wealthy lawyer, academic and collector, Basilius Amerbach (1533–91), which it placed on display to the public from 1671. Yet, it functioned primarily as a research library and had little place for exhibition space as museums do today.

Some historians regard the Ashmolean Museum, Oxford, as the first public museum.[18] The collections of natural history and ethnography that eventually formed the Ashmolean Museum were formed by John Tradescant the elder (1570–1638) and his son, John Tradescant the younger (1608–62), gardeners to King Charles I in the early 17th century.[19] Their Musaeum Tradescantianum was displayed in a large house, 'The Ark', in Lambeth, London where it could be viewed by members of the public for sixpence.[20] Upon Tradescant's death the collection passed to wealthy politician and antiquarian Elias Ashmole (1617–92), who gifted the collection to the University of Oxford on the condition that a suitable building was provided in which to show it to the public (duly opened in 1683).[21] Admission fees varied: most visitors between 1683 and 1697 paid one shilling, although the fee was sometimes as low as sixpence.[22]

Other historians will name the Capitoline Museums, Rome, as the world's oldest collections of art intended to be shown to the public. The collection of classical statuary was initially begun by Pope Sixtus IV in the 1470s as the papal collection of art and was enlarged by subsequent gifts from later Popes. It eventually opened as a museum for the public in the 18th century. The origins of the famous Uffizi Gallery in Florence can also be traced to this period: the collections of Francesco de Medici, second Grand Duke of Tuscany (1541–87) and Ferdinando, third Grand Duke of Tuscany (1549–1609) were open for certain members of the public to visit from 1582, although only by special request.

Thus, while the Ashmolean may be the first permanent public exhibition founded for the benefit of academics, scholars and students, it is possible to argue that the foundations of the Capitoline Museums' collections lie in the 15th century. Yet, if we consider that a museum must be a 'non-profit, permanent institution in the service of society and its development, open to the public',[23] then the first true 'museum' in Europe must be an institution fully open to all members of the public, rather than a select and privileged few, and this development only occurred from the mid-18th century as national museums began to be founded.

The founding of national museums in Europe

By the 1750s the British government had begun to consider that it had a responsibility to establish an institution to preserve and maintain a collection open to the public. Upon his death in 1753, the physician and naturalist Sir Hans Sloane offered to leave his large and impressive collection of coins, medals, books, prints, manuscripts, a herbarium, and 'things related to the customs of ancient times' to the 'nation of England', on the condition that the government compensate his heirs and provide facilities to house and maintain the collections. His collection, and those of Sir Robert Cotton (1570–1631) and Robert Harley, 1st Earl of Oxford (1661–1724), eventually became the foundation of the British Museum when in 1753 Parliament issued an Act stating that these collections were to be 'preserved and maintained, not only for the Inspection and Entertainment of the Learned and the Curious, but for the General

Use and Benefit of the Publick'.[24] The museum was opened to the public in 1759 and admission was free of charge, although only a limited number of tickets were issued each day, requiring an application in advance.[25]

The example of the British Museum was replicated all over Europe in the 18th and 19th centuries. As enlightened ideas of liberty and equality took hold, monarchies and governments came under increased pressure to enable public access to royal collections, or to found public museums sponsored by the state or monarchy. The story of the foundation of many national museums is also linked closely to the development of national consciousness as well as mass enfranchisement all over Europe in the 19th century.

Museums in the 19th century

The 1840s to the 1890s saw an extraordinary rise in the creation and building of public museums throughout Europe, which has been referred to as 'the Museum Age'. The development of the public museum coincided with the growth of other public institutions or attractions such as department stores, public parks and world expositions, as well as a growth in the travel and tourism industry. Many believed museums could provide instruction, education, entertainment, and assist in instilling a degree of discipline among populations.[26] In an age which valued philanthropy and civic pride, the founding of museums by national and regional authorities was intended to serve the public good and was widespread throughout Europe.

In Britain, the wish by many of those in government to enact social reforms to overcome problems resulting from industrialisation and overpopulation in urban areas contributed to the development of public museums. The 1845 the Museums Act (or the 'Act for Encouraging the Establishment of Museums in Large Towns') was an important development for the history of museums in Britain: now, local authorities were permitted to levy a small tax to set up and support museums.[27] Furthermore, research in archaeology and anthropology particularly thrived in this period and academics established networks of collaborators among missionaries, travellers, and colonial officials in order to gather objects, images and information relating to indigenous peoples and histories all over the world. It was considered important to assemble such objects alongside information and material relating to the British and European past and to display them to a public. In addition, many regional museums of archaeology, geology or natural history were also established in the 19th century in Britain by learned societies founded by the newly educated and wealthy middle classes.[28] By the start of the First World War, most large towns in Britain had a municipal museum, the objects to be held by the local authority in trust forever.[29]

Museums today

The number of museums in the world has risen greatly since the middle of the 20th century: perhaps as many as three new museums opened every week in the UK in the 1980s; museums in China have grown from about 1,400 at the outset of the 21st century to over 5,000 today and in the last 10 years there has been a significant investment in numerous new 'mega museums' in the Middle East.[30] Numbers of staff employed by museums in the UK also rose markedly in the late 20th century and membership of ICOM grew from 1,000 in 1974 to around 180,000 by 2006.[31] It is difficult to generalise about how many members of staff a small, medium or large museum may have, and even harder to estimate how many people work in museums worldwide at any one time. Staff in museums might work full-time or part-time, on fixed-term or permanent contracts, and might be paid or unpaid; volunteers play a large and important part in the workforce for most museums.

Museums must necessarily work within the political and economic framework of the nation and region in which they operate. This means the political and financial support they receive will fluctuate and they must establish ways of working and approaches that can assist in overcoming the inevitable changes.[32] Many museums have attempted to apply management structures and ways of working akin to those found in the corporate sector, implementing measures through which to strengthen themselves within the leisure and entertainment industry.[33] This includes the creation of corporate plans, direction and goals, the introduction of additional and more diverse methods of income generation, and department restructuring and rationalisation.[34]

The way museums operate is frequently tied to government policy: national guidelines defining what a museum is, what it should do, and what support it might receive, are present in many countries and museums are encouraged to follow them.[35] These policies and guidelines are heavily informed by international sector standards, devised by organisations such as ICOM. Yet, formal national legislation relating to, and regulation of, museums is not present in all countries of the world and can vary in nature and specificity. Some countries operate national registration schemes, and organisations must become accredited in order to be recognised as official museums. The criteria and process for registration or accreditation varies from country to country, and the schemes can be administered either by the national government or an appointed independent institute. In the USA, for example, the American Alliance of Museums runs an accreditation scheme and in the UK the accreditation scheme is administered by Arts Council England.[36] ICOM has established its own *Code of Ethics for Museums*, setting out the most important professional standards and levels of performance museums should be operating under.[37] These principles act as guidelines for those working in museums, and should be used to inform the work of any museum:

- Museums preserve, interpret and promote the natural and cultural inheritance of humanity.
- Museums that maintain collections hold them in trust for the benefit of society and its development.
- Museums hold primary evidence for establishing and furthering knowledge.
- Museums provide opportunities for the appreciation, understanding and management of the natural and cultural heritage.
- Museums hold resources that provide opportunities for other public services and benefits.
- Museums work in close collaboration with the communities from which their collections originate as well as those they serve.
- Museums operate in a legal manner.
- Museums operate in a professional manner.

Types of museums

The size (not only of the collections, but also the building(s) and the staff), type, activity, purpose and intended audiences of museums can vary considerably, from large national museums that receive government subsidies, open every day of the week and with defined departments, to volunteer-run independent trusts with limited space, relying on private donations to open once a week.

Museums can be categorised according to their foundation, funding or governance:

- National museums: receive partial funding from central government.
- Local-authority funded museums: certain funding is awarded by local government authorities.
- Trusts and charities: receive income from donations and fundraising.
- Independent museums: may be run in a manner more akin to a corporate organisation.
- University museums: overseen by a university, which may fund all or part of the running costs.
- Corporate museums: owned and run by a corporation.
- Military museums: funded in part by a military corps or regiment.

Museums can also be classified according to the area they serve (for example, national, local, regional, rural, urban); by whom they are aiming to serve (general public, specialist audiences, younger audiences); and by the method through which their collections are displayed and interpreted (with an emphasis on interactivity and technology, diorama or period room, arrangements that are systematic, thematic or contemplative, or experiences taking place in the 'open air'). The founding principles, mission and staff of one museum may be more closely focussed on research and education, whereas another institution might be more eager to entertain and encourage participation.[38]

A collection is at the core of the majority of museums and another way to categorise a museum is by the nature of that collection:

- History or social history museums: objects relating to a specific society, person, place or period. These collections may include archaeological material, natural history specimens and human remains.
- Ethnographic museums: objects that assist in the study of people and culture, perhaps grouped according to place or people.
- Natural history museums: animal, plant and geological specimens, perhaps also human remains. Objects might be from particular geographic areas or time periods.

- Science and technology museums: objects that assist in the study of subjects relating to the sciences. Some science 'museums' may not have many (or any) objects and may be considered as science centres.
- Art museums: artworks from many different time periods, styles, and places, executed by many different schools of art and artists.
- Historic built environment and natural landscapes: sometimes considered distinct from museums, though many still contain historic objects and offer experiences akin to history museums. An historic building may be considered as an 'object' in itself.

Quite often museums will contain a variety of different collections and embrace a number of fields.

What do museums do?

As the preceding section has shown, many museums began as collections of beautiful and curious objects belonging to private, privileged individuals. By the 19th and 20th centuries the word museum came to mean a building housing objects of cultural, historic or natural significance, which the public could access. Historically, many museums were established as a result of the wish to research and understand people, cultures, ideas and concepts through the focussed and in-depth study of historic objects: this emphasis on collecting, preservation, study, display and interpretation of objects still pervades our definition of what constitutes a museum today.

Ideas about what role museums must play in society, and the value they have, frequently change. We might, for example, consider that museums belong to the wider entertainment and leisure industry, competing with other entertainment facilities such as theatres, cinemas and shopping centres. By the 1990s, museums in the UK began to suffer from reductions in funding, and many began to seek ways to support and reinvigorate their work through a more business-oriented approach.[39] This led to many museums taking steps to 'commodify' their assets, monetise their products (research and expertise, exhibitions, public programmes and spaces as venues for hire) and focus on attracting greater numbers of visitors through targeted marketing and PR and audience evaluation.[40] Some have suggested that museums have moved too far away from their role as organisations offering educative experiences, commodifying the 'relics and events of the past' for consumption in a consumer society.[41]

One of the major roles of museums traditionally has been that of education: the museum can be a valuable place for informal learning outside of the classroom, where enquiry, exploration and self-directed learning are encouraged. Most museums will have education goals and objectives: maintaining this kind of educational role is perhaps what sets the museum apart from 'commercial, theme-park heritage', which could be classed as popular entertainment, rather than education.[42]

Museums also have a role in inspiring visitors, as arenas in which visitors can connect to their emotions, reflect and develop in other ways than intellectually. Museums can bring social, political and cultural developments to the attention of the public and encourage thoughtful, stimulating and respectful conversations about them, perhaps inspiring evocative and emotional responses: 'safe places for unsafe ideas'.[43] If we return to the history of the museum and recall the nature of the Mouseion in Alexandria the similarities with today's museums as centres of learning, exploration and public discussion are clear.

Who museums are for and who they represent is a complex, important and challenging issue, one which cannot be discussed in depth in this publication. Demands made on museums change frequently as a result of national and regional priorities and policies and museums must continually justify their position.[44] They must also actively seek to involve and engage the public in their activities, and ensure this public is as broad and diverse as possible. In the late 20th century the museums sector experienced a change: at this time many people began to question why museums were catering primarily (or in some cases exclusively) for elite audiences, representing only a small percentage of the total population.[45] A new critical approach to museums began to form: the New Museology movement.[46] Traditional ways of presenting collections and ideas were called into question and calls were made for museums to make themselves accessible to more people.[47] These issues are examined in more detail in Chapters 8 and 9.

The social, cultural and economic value of museums

Museums can play an important part in encouraging and maintaining any country's social, cultural and economic development. These institutions that collect and preserve evidence of a society's cultural and natural heritage can help communities, places and whole nations to explore identity and belonging and help them to consider and construct possible futures.[48] This role in the construction and maintenance of identity is a powerful argument for the value of any museum in society.[49]

Other social benefits of museums are not difficult to identify: they can act as a focus for the community; lead or support in the organisation and hosting of cultural events and activities; and promote and provide varied opportunities for volunteering programmes, community activities or training programmes.[50] Social and physical regeneration of an area or community may well be bound-up with such undertakings. As venues in which visitors can feel enriched and welcomed, and as places in which they might experience validation, guidance and a sense of well-being, museums offer valuable experiences for the social development of individuals, groups and whole communities.[51] This role as a public service assisting in the social welfare of individuals, groups and communities has become increasingly important to museums in recent times.

Museums often play a role in economic development, rural and urban regeneration and are recognised as tourist attractions. Indeed, this role of museums and heritage sites as 'places of consumption' that encourage development and investment around them is why many continue to attract funding.[52] The formation of new communities or the regeneration and redevelopment of an area may well include plans for cultural facilities like museums.

2 Collecting policies, composition and implementation

This chapter will examine how and what museums might collect. A logical way to begin is to consider what is meant by a collector, and what it means to collect. An understanding of the nature of collecting, history of collecting, and the different ways collections have been used and presented in museums can be beneficial to the work of a curator, enabling them to more fully understand the history and development of the collections they care for.

In contrast to an accumulator, a collector actively acquires objects that are of particular interest to them and that carry symbolic meaning. A collector will also rationalise their purchases with a variety of explanations and order or arrange their collection in some way.[1] A collector may also be eager for contemporaries to view their collection as a way through which to advertise their discrimination and taste. Once collected in this way, objects take on subjective status and symbolic meanings and, if no longer utilised, they can be possessed.[2] Sociologist and cultural theorist Jean Baudrillard notes the fact that the former function of an object is usually immaterial to a collector: that an old stamp can be put on a letter or an old car be driven becomes far less important than possessing the object itself, divested of its function.[3] Furthermore, when collected, objects will often gain social meaning, for example, implying status, prestige or wealth. Collectors themselves will attach 'moral and economic values' to objects, which may help to shape their identities and bring significance to their lives.[4] Generally, one object will never be enough for a collector: an object can only function via its relationship with others and a whole succession is usually required. As Susan Pearce identifies, objects are socially meaningful but 'their meaning is produced by arranging them in sets, both mentally and physically'.[5] Sometimes owning an entire set of objects will become the goal for a collector, the completion of that set signifying the accomplishment of a 'mission'.[6]

Why we collect

Collecting of objects takes place both inside and outside of the museum for many reasons:[7]

- Collecting can be motivated by scholarly interests: a collector might be an historian and wish to build a collection of objects that have historical and cultural significance and associations. They might carry out research on the objects and use this to add to knowledge on a subject, person or time period.
- Collecting can bring pleasure, satisfying an aesthetic desire, as well as a need for possession. The possession and the creation of a collection offers an opportunity to escape, and to 'abolish time' or 'translate real time into the dimensions of a system'.[8]
- Some collectors use their collections and collecting activity to enhance their self-definition, perhaps to bring more meaning to their lives and form an identity for themselves.
- Collections may be a means to bring order and structure to a collector's life.[9] As Baudrillard suggests: 'for while the object is a resistant material, it is also simultaneously, a mental realm over which I hold sway, a thing whose meaning is governed by myself alone'.[10]
- The inclination to collect can also be as a result of pure acquisitiveness. As John Elsner and Roger Cardinal find,

'as one becomes conscious of one's self, one becomes a conscious collector of identity, projecting one's being onto the objects one chooses to live with. Taste, the collector's taste, is a mirror of self.'[11]

- Collecting can be a socially acceptable form of spending and consumption, and art objects in particular are considered as relatively straightforward and secure forms of investment. There may be an aim to achieve some financial benefit from the sale of objects at a later date.
- Collecting can be motivated by competition: a result of the desire to extend one's business activities from 'the boardroom and marketplace to the auction gallery and drawing room.'[12] Linked to this is a desire for immortality: some individuals aim to create a collection because they hope it will survive after their death and retain their memory.
- The collecting of objects can often be motivated by the wish to express ideas or attributes of taste and social status, which might assist in achieving further social advancement. The term 'conspicuous consumption', first coined in the 19th century, is now commonly used to describe the purchase and acquisition of luxury goods or services in order to display one's economic success and power. As this kind of display is usually made in public, it becomes a method of increasing social position or maintaining a particular status and making a declaration of personal wealth. Sociologist Pierre Bourdieu's research into the ways in which cultural tastes arise out of, and are mobilised in, struggles for social recognition or status is important to consider when we think about why individuals might collect certain kinds of objects.[13] His sociology of cultural consumption asserts that attempts to retain social status by the dominant classes often involve practices that emphasise and exhibit cultural distinctions and differences.[14] Cultural capital can play a significant role in power relations in societies: cultural symbols and categories are frequently used as instruments of power, providing 'the means for a non-economic form of domination and hierarchy, as classes distinguish themselves through taste.'[15]
- Collecting may be undertaken as a result of a preoccupation with the past, and with provenance or reputation. Through certain objects a collector may be able to identify with the past and

associate themselves with famous historical figures or particular moments in history. This may be connected to attempts to enhance their status or reputation.

Different collectors will approach their collecting in different ways. Their collecting activity might be haphazard, driven by curiosity or personal interest and meaning. It might also be 'fetishist', with the collector being concerned to collect as many examples of the same or similar objects as possible. Finally, it might be systematic, with the collector building up objects in a comprehensive and deliberate way using a planned and measured approach, perhaps even to illustrate a particular point of view or idea.[16] When such distinctions like these are drawn we make moral judgements about the collecting activity of others: society can often deem some kinds of collecting as more worthy than others.[17]

Collecting is a culturally charged and significant activity: it is an interaction between humans and material culture, not just the gathering of objects.[18] An important conclusion to make regarding collecting as a cultural system (and particularly when considering collections in museums), is that eventually a collection becomes part of a broader project or arena, is confronted by others, and constitutes itself as a message.[19]

How museums collect

Collections cultivated by the efforts of individuals, for one or more of the reasons listed above, may eventually form the basis of a museum.[20] As Chapter 1 has shown, the first museums were formed from collections of objects that were valued and considered worthy of study and display to the public for educational reasons. Collecting remains one of the primary activities of museums today and is often what sets museums apart from other organisations in the leisure sector.[21]

Objects in museum collections are usually those that are valued by people in some way, and have been moved from their original locations and collected together with a specific purpose, generally to be preserved and kept in the museum forever.[22] These groupings of objects within the museum will be imbued with some kind of meaning, and may be used to transmit certain messages and reinforce cultural traditions.[23] There are several reasons why a museum collection might be created over time:

- Rescuing groups of objects: sometimes entire groups of objects are in danger of being destroyed or purchased by private owners, and might be 'rescued', forming a museum. Additional objects may then be added over time.
- To create a new museum: groups of people or organisations might actively acquire objects to fulfil a particular purpose.
- To fill gaps in the collections of an existing museum or develop it in new ways.
- For display needs: perhaps for temporary exhibitions or new programming.
- For research purposes: for example, scientific sampling for natural history or ethnographic museums.

Museums acquire objects in a variety of ways:

- Purchase: this is a proactive approach to collecting, purchases will usually be made to complement the existing collections, or to fill gaps. Museums are invariably restricted in what they can purchase by the funds they have available and not all will have the ability to make purchases.
- Active acquisition, without charge: objects might be collected by museum staff or affiliates, without a purchase being made. In such situations it is important to ensure all relevant permissions are in place and documentation retained.
- Collecting in the field: many natural history museums and museums with large amounts of archaeological or ethnographic material have a remit to accept newly discovered items. This systematic approach to collecting is usually part of a wider research and collecting programme.
- Exchange with other museums: objects might be offered to another institution so that they might be more appropriately cared for and displayed in alternative locations (usually only other non-profit organisations, not private individuals).
- Donation: objects might be gifted to the museum during a collector's lifetime, or upon their death as a bequest. The scale and form of donations to museums varies widely. In some countries there are incentives to private collectors donating objects to

museums: a reduction in inheritance taxes for example.[24] Not all donations to museums will be accepted however (see Chapter 3).

- Loan: objects might be loaned from individuals or other museums to benefit and improve the collections, or for short-term exhibitions or special programming.

There have been periods when museums were able and willing to collect at great speed. National museums in the late 18th and early 19th centuries in Europe were often formed from the core collection of an individual, which was then added to apace, often in order to show 'possession and mastery' of the world.[25] Due to a loss of funds and expertise, such mass accumulation is no longer possible for many museums. Yet museums should continue to actively and systematically add to their collections.[26]

Collecting mandates

No museum can collect everything: generally, museums have limited space, budgets and staff numbers, so a programme of collecting should be adopted that is realistic, specific and achievable.[27] Consideration should be given to which staff should be undertaking the activity; how much time they should be spending on it; what funds there are available for the work; and the implications for future care and display of the potential new objects.[28] A museum that continually accepts any and all objects it is offered risks losing its appeal, and a great deal of time and money will need to be spent caring for collections that may never be seen by the public.[29] A collecting policy that enables a museum to define its identity and purpose is more likely to attract visitors and helps the museum to remain relevant to a particular society or audiences.[30]

Collections that have been managed by one person, or by patchy and changeable collecting policies, perhaps affected by stakeholder pressure or fads and whims, engineered to express the world views of particular individuals or ruling groups, will invariably contain gaps and inconsistencies.[31] A museum should therefore compose and adopt a written Collections Development Policy (CDP) to ensure what it collects can assist in accomplishing its overall mission.[32] ICOM advocates this approach in its *Code of Ethics for Museums*, section 2.1 Collections Policy.[33]

Collections development policies

A museum's Collections Development Policy (CDP) forms part of its Collections Management Policy (CMP). More information on CMPs can be found in Chapter 4, Collections Management Policies. A CDP will help museums to recognise what objects they have, identify any gaps, and state what they will collect in the future, with reference to the available resources of the organisation.[34] Such a policy will outline the specific development care, use and management of a collection for a five- to ten-year period, and will include information on:

- The museum's purpose, its mission and governance.
- The legal constraints and ethical guidelines that the museum operates within.
- The date on which the CDP was approved by the museum's governing body and the review process and date.
- What objects the museum already has and how they are used.
- The historical background of the formation of the existing collections.
- The strengths and weaknesses of the collections. What gaps there might be and how they might be addressed.
- Why the museum should collect in certain fields, and why these particular objects (i.e. how they help to fulfil the museum's mission).
- The museum's vision for the collections moving forward and how this will meet the aims of the museum.
- How the collections might be developed to serve particular existing or underrepresented audiences or communities.
- The resources that already exist to care for and display the collections (space, staff, materials, budgets).
- Whether these resources will continue to be available, and what else might be required in the future if collecting continues.
- How the museum's objects can be preserved adequately to ensure they survive for the future with the existing and predicted resources that will be available.
- How the museum will consider loans to the collections, and the criteria and requirements for these.
- The criteria for acquisition resulting from the above information, forming the museum's Acquisitions Policy.

- The museum's rationalisation plans/priorities and Deaccessions Policy (for more on these last two policies see Chapter 3, Researching and accessioning new collection objects).

A Collections Development Policy forms part of high-level policy-making in a museum, and it should be part of the museum's management policy and forward plan. It must contain as much detail as possible and be approved by the governing body of the museum. All staff within the museum must be informed of the existence of such a policy, and it should be made widely available. Periodic reviews of the policy are important, in order to assess its effectiveness and continued relevance.

Legal and ethical restrictions on collecting

The illegal trade of valuable and significant objects, stolen from owners or taken without permission from archaeological sites, or from a country in contravention of local and national legislation, has existed for centuries.[35] Many countries across the world pass and enforce legislation which protects and controls the movement of culturally important objects via both legal and illegal trade. The range, variety and extent of such legislation varies from country to country. Acquiring objects through gift, purchase, bequest and fieldwork for museums or individual collections can be fraught with difficulties and there will always be certain legal and ethical restrictions that must be observed.[36] Every museum should be operating within the principles set out by ICOM for the acquisition of objects in its *Code of Ethics for Museum*.[37]

In 1970, the United Nations Educational, Scientific and Cultural Organization (UNESCO) established the Convention on the Means of Prohibiting and Preventing the Illicit Export, Import and Transfer of Ownership of Cultural Property.[38] In 1995, this was strengthened by the UNIDROIT Convention on Stolen or Illegally Exported Cultural Objects. This international treaty aimed to tackle the illegal trade in cultural artefacts and was recognised by UNESCO member states. These conventions require members to put in place, and to follow, measures that oppose the illegal movement of cultural property (defined as 'those which, on religious or secular grounds, are of importance for archaeology, prehistory, history, literature, art or science').[39] This includes, for example, checking the legitimacy of purchases, returning objects that can be shown to have been illegally exported, monitoring trade, imposing penal sanctions and returning objects that can be shown to be essential parts of a country's cultural or natural heritage.[40] The Conventions are not, however, retroactive and the terms only apply to objects deemed as stolen or illegally exported after 1970.

Other major international legislation aiming to reduce the illegal trade and destruction of cultural artefacts includes:

- Convention for the Protection of Cultural Property in the Event of Armed Conflict (the Hague Convention), 1954, Protocol [now First Protocol], 1954 and Second Protocol, 1999.
- Convention on International Trade in Endangered Species of Wild Fauna and Flora (1973).
- UN Convention on Biological Diversity (1992).
- UNIDROIT Convention on Stolen and Illegally Exported Cultural Objects (1995).
- UNESCO Convention on the Protection of the Underwater Cultural Heritage (2001).
- UNESCO Convention for the Safeguarding of the Intangible Cultural Heritage (2003).

Not all countries of the world have ratified the conventions, yet the policies of any museum should recognise their existence and reflect the recommendations.[41]

Museums must be proactive in establishing the provenance and legal ownership of objects before they enter their collections in order to avoid acquiring objects that have been stolen, illegally obtained, illegally exported, or illegally removed from a protected site.[42] The donor or seller of an object must be able to show that they acquired the object legally, and the museum must be satisfied that transferring ownership will not contravene any international or national legislation.[43]

Collecting sensitive material

The early origins of European museums examined in Chapter 1 shows that many museums' collections were formed in the 18th and 19th centuries at a time when world travel by wealthy and scholarly individuals was increasingly possible. This was also a time when many European nations were seeking to extend their authority over other peoples and territories in the wider world, through colonisation. Such activities often resulted in objects from other nations and peoples being removed from their countries of origin and placed in European museums.

This movement, and assumed ownership, of material culture was sometimes carried out legitimately, through purchase or gift. Frequently, however, objects were removed without the agreement of the source nation or people. Accumulating the material culture of the colonised countries enabled Europeans to assert their supposed superiority, and to express their distinctiveness in an age of developing nationalism. Stories presented in museums allowed Western nations to recreate particular versions of their own pasts, in attempts to legitimise their positions.[44] As a result, the origins of many collections in Western museums are rooted in colonialism, with museums established and collecting funding through the profits of imperialism.[45]

Today, in a postcolonial and post-imperial age, museums are becoming more aware of, and more eager to acknowledge and discuss, these events of the past and the controversial origins of some of their collections.[46] As well as acknowledging these issues, many museums are also trying to tackle the challenge of decolonising their institutions and there has been a significant rise in initiatives, campaigns and exhibitions devoted to decolonising museums over the past ten years. The meaning of decolonisation is heavily debated, and some authors feel that European museums will never fully achieve it, considering the foundations of many are so deeply rooted in empire.[47] Decolonising the museum should involve:

- Acknowledging the colonial past; thinking critically about how this past affects the present operations and activities of the museum, but also of wider society.
- Recognising the role of museums as caretakers of non-Western material culture.
- Taking steps to be more accountable towards source communities.

- Considering the legacies colonialism has left, not just on the content of the museum's displays, but also on operations, staffing and governance, and making changes in these areas.[48]

As a minimum, museums must work closely with communities connected to the objects of non-Western cultures to ensure they are accessible to them and that authority for their care, display and interpretation is shared.[49]

This debate also extends to the consideration of the return of museum objects to source nations and communities. This can be a highly controversial and emotive issue, one that is often fiercely debated.[50] There are many issues to consider, including the legality of the acquisition of the object(s), their importance to academic or scientific research, and the care and security of the object(s) if it is returned to the country of origin.[51] The 21st century has seen a shift in policy: museums are now much more likely to consider issues of repatriation and work in partnership with those affected by the issues.[52] Every request for repatriation made to a museum should be assessed individually, on a case-by-case basis: different museums have different policies and procedures and, unfortunately, the outcome may not please all interested parties.[53] Yet repatriation (or restitution) is an increasingly common practice and some museums have agreed to return objects with cultural and religious significance, or human remains and sacred objects, to their countries of origin.

The collection and display of human remains in museums, is another challenging and sensitive issue with multiple philosophical, legal and ethical dimensions.[54] In the past, some museums may have treated human remains as just another kind of object within their collections. Today, there is a recognition in most organisations that human remains should be accorded special treatment in their display and storage.[55] In the UK, the treatment of human remains by museums has altered significantly in the 21st century and many organisations have begun to remove them from their collections and return them to the country of origin.[56] There are strong arguments on both sides of this debate, and the process for deaccessioning such objects is not straightforward. In the UK a full statement of good practice in this area for museums was published in 2005 by the Department for Digital, Culture, Media and Sport.[57] In many nations, similar legislation is now in force, including, for example, the Native American Graves Protection and Repatriation Act 1990 (NAGPRA) in the US, and the Aboriginal and Torres Strait Islander Heritage Protection Act 1984 in Australia. The approaches of different museums to this issue will vary and each organisation should devise a thorough policy containing information on the extent of the collections; future collecting intentions; storage, conservation, public access and display of the collections; and the processes for considering repatriation requests.

Collections rationalisation

Most museums do not have enough space to adequately display (or even store) everything they have: large collections that have been allowed to grow to fill all available space pose major problems for collections care and expenditure. The periodic reassessment and reduction of collection objects is a necessary part of a curator's work as museums continue to think about the messages they construct and the nature and quality of the collections they care for.[58] This reassessment might be done through rehousing, reorganising, redistributing or (re)cataloguing.

The act of deaccession is the permanent removal of objects from a museum's collection. The process can be complex, often risky, and sometimes even unethical. Generally, a museum acquires objects with the intention of retaining them in perpetuity and so removing objects from a collection is controversial. In the simplest sense, removing objects from a collection might be viewed as highly disrespectful to the efforts of donors or original founders of the museum who bequeathed or purchased them in the first place, and also to museum audiences who wish to view them.[59] There may even be legal reasons why objects cannot be removed from certain collections, indeed deaccessioning objects from designated museum collections is forbidden in many countries across the world. The disposal of objects has also been considered by some museums as a way of alleviating financial problems or improving the quality of the collections.[60]

It is, however, important for museums to consider how their present collections fit into their overall collecting mandate. In some countries, museums are permitted to employ deaccessioning as a way to strengthen their positions (for example, the UK and USA). Museum collections grow and change over time and, if carefully considered and officially managed, deaccessioning can sometimes play a part in effective collections management.[61] If deaccessioning is legally permitted by the country in which a museum operates, it might consider disposing of an object because:

- It has decayed or been damaged so badly that it cannot be conserved or repaired and is no longer of use in display or teaching etc. Opinions from object-specialists and conservators should be sought to clarify this.
- It no longer fits into the museum's collecting remit and is no longer relevant to the museum's purpose and mission. Collecting patterns can be influenced by fashions, so caution should be applied.
- The museum does not have the resources to properly care for the object.
- There are several similar or identical examples of the object in the collection in better condition, or with more information known about them. Though it is possible that, in time, more information about the object might be uncovered.
- It can be exchanged with a better quality or type of object from another museum in order to strengthen the collections.
- It has been discovered to be a fake, a forgery, a copy, or to have a different identity than originally thought. However, even if fake, an object may still be of interest, or have some other importance.
- It will be returned to the country or people from which it originated (see above: Collecting sensitive material).
- It can be sold in order to make money for the museum or to buy 'better' objects. This is a highly controversial practice and is contrary to the founding principles of most museums. Sometimes museums are ordered by local or state governments or departments to sell objects, and in such cases there is often little a museum can do to resist such instructions.[62] In the UK, the Museums Association's *Code of Ethics* calls on museums to 'refuse to undertake disposal principally for financial reasons, except where it will significantly improve the long-term public benefit derived from the remaining collection.'[63]

Some museums decide never to sell or exchange any objects, some only dispose of objects to other public collections, and still others freely sell or exchange objects in order to enhance their collections and release funds to care for existing objects.[64] When deaccessioning does happen, and it is decided that the objects are to be sold, it is generally accepted that the proceeds should be used to benefit the museum's other objects, or its collecting and conservation activities (see ICOM's *Code of Ethics for Museums*, 2.16).[65] As this area of museum practice often comes under intense public scrutiny, museums must ensure that decisions surrounding deaccessioning are made only after informed, full and careful discussion and consultation and with reference to relevant legal and ethical frameworks and guidelines, and the particular policies and processes of the museum.[66] These frameworks might be ones that apply to all public bodies, or that exist particularly in relation to museums. If deaccessioning is undertaken, there are certain ethical conditions and procedures that should be observed (see Chapter 3, Deaccessions policies). The entire deaccessioning process should be rigorously documented, and the outcome carefully communicated to stakeholders and the public.[67]

Loans

Many museums will consider loaning their objects to other organisations. Museums usually only lend objects from their collections to similar institutions, ones that can provide appropriate transport provisions, storage and display conditions, and security for vulnerable and valuable museum objects. It is usually important that organisations borrowing objects from a museum should advance their use in publicly accessible projects or for research, and not seek to make profit from the objects.[68]

Many museums will borrow objects for short-term projects such as special exhibitions or defined programming. There should always be a connection between the loan of an object into the museum and its overall mission. Museums should not borrow objects from private individuals if this might cause a conflict of interest (for example, a commission or fee would be received, or the exhibition of an object in a museum is intended to enhance its value).[69] If a loan is no longer needed it must be returned: this will help to avoid the object having to be cared for and stored by the museum for no benefit.

Museums should devise their own policies in this area, setting out the criteria and limitations of loans in and out of the organisation (see Chapter 4, Loans policies).

Contemporary collecting

Often, the collecting policy of a museum will focus on the acquisition of historic objects. This can often mean that museums miss out on collecting objects of the present. More and more museums are collecting things of today that may be historically significant tomorrow, and many museums now have clear and purposeful policies aiming to ensure significant and representative contemporary objects do not disappear. Contemporary collecting allows museums to document technological and social transformations that are already underway, and to make acquisitions that reflect modern life.[70] It is also motivated by the fact that today's museum visitors are increasingly eager to see themselves reflected in the content of displays and activities. Furthermore, instead of simply confining efforts to collect expensive and impressive objects of the past, museums are now taking positive steps to preserve those commonplace, typical and more popular objects, in order to create more representative and balanced collections.

This undertaking is not easy and can be risky. Curators need to become skilled in gauging which objects from the contemporary scene might be of interest to historians and the public in the future. The later value of objects in a museum can be hard to predict and careful decisions must be made. There is always a risk to accessioning something into a collection, especially when budgets are small, and space is limited. It is important for a curator to undertake sufficient research in order to gather information about potential new acquisitions before making a decision. Another challenge of objects of modern times is that they are more likely to be disposable in nature and have an ephemerality that poses challenges for storage, preservation and conservation. Furthermore, how to collect digital objects, and ensure we do not lose such 'objects' in the digital age remains an important developing area of curatorship.

PART TWO

MANAGING COLLECTIONS

3 Researching and accessioning new collection objects

Acquisition is the term used when a museum obtains an object, and this chapter will discuss the various processes through which museums acquire objects and then make them part of their collections. A museum may acquire objects in many different ways, from different sources, and in a variety of quantities. Whether the objects will then be accepted as part of the permanent collections of the museum may have been decided in advance, or this might be determined after the object is acquired.[1]

Acquisitions policies

A museum's Acquisitions Policy forms part of its Collections Development Policy (CDP: see Chapter 2). It is intended to help a museum shape its collections by outlining what it should acquire and how.[2]

It should cover things like:

- The procedure and appropriate level of authority for accepting objects.
- The type of objects the museum should collect, in what disciplines, and relating to which subjects and thematic areas.
- The geographical and chronological extent and limits of collecting.
- The level of significance of the objects to be collected (for example, individual, local, national, relating to a person or a place).
- How the museum should collect: through purchase, donation or fieldwork.[3]

Additionally, the policy may include questions that staff involved in collecting should ask before agreeing to acquire an object:

- If the legal ownership and provenance of the object can be adequately established.
- If an object fulfils certain conditions relating to provenance or association set out by the museum.
- If the gift, bequest or sale comes with any particular conditions.
- If the object is in good enough condition to be of use to the museum and survive for the future.
- If there are any extra copyright, safety and security implications in acquiring the object.
- If the museum can adequately care for the object with the current levels of staff, funding and exhibition or storage space available.
- How useful the object can be to the museum's activities in research, education, exhibition, or if there is a danger the object will end up in storage forever, or eventually be deaccessioned.
- If there are many of the same items in the collection already, and this object would simply be duplication.
- If enough is known about the object and if a good level of documentation can be provided for it.
- If the object is particularly unusual or significant for it to present an exceptional opportunity for the museum, so be considered as a special case for acquisition, even if it does not meet some of the other criteria noted above.

A comprehensive acquisitions policy will assist the museum in collecting only the objects that will help it to achieve its mission (i.e. ones that can be actively used) and that it can feasibly care for. It is for this reason that many museums publish their Acquisitions Policy on their website so that potential donors and sellers can find out what the museum will and will not accept.[4] The policy should be formally approved by the museum's governing body and reviewed periodically (at least once every five years).

The acquisitions process

That museums acquire objects via donation, purchase, collecting in the field, or loan, has been discussed in Chapter 2, How museums collect. The process for considering whether an object should be accepted into the museum's collection, and how it should be formally accessioned, is similar in each case.

DONATIONS (GIFTS)

Objects offered to museums as gifts should be given freely by the owners and financial (or any other kind of) compensation should not be offered. It is important that the donation is formally recorded, and an agreement is signed by both the museum and the donor to reflect the complete and unconditional delivery of the objects.[5] The following is a typical process for considering and accepting gifts:

- An offer is made by a donor. This is communicated to the appropriate museum staff.
- The offer is investigated, and a note made of the details, in an offer record (see below, Offer or potential purchase record).
- The object is examined, and information about it gathered and recorded.
- The object is considered with reference to the museum's Collections Development Policy.
- A decision-making process is undertaken, through consultation with museum staff or via an established Collections Development Committee.
- A decision is made, and the donor is formally notified.

- If the donation is refused, the museum formally thanks the donor and suggests other potential repositories.
- If the donation is accepted, the museum issues a formal letter of thanks stating the conditions under which the object is being accepted by the museum.
- The museum takes possession of the object and gathers as much information about it as possible (see Chapter 4, Object biographies).
- Entry documentation is completed (see below, Entry process).
- The object is inspected, and any necessary conservation or treatment is undertaken.
- A catalogue record and object file are created (see Chapter 4, Collections Documentation Policies, Plans and Procedures).

Sometimes curators must deal with unsolicited donations, objects left at the museum without permission and lacking any accompanying information and documentation. Often unarranged and unannounced donations are not accessioned by museums because the objects do not fit into their Collections Development Policies, or do not have any associated records of provenance to verify their legal ownership.[6] When such objects are discovered, every effort should be made to identify the donor and record any information about them.

Similarly, sometimes donations are offered to museums with certain conditions attached. For example, some donors might wish to retain partial ownership of the donation, or for the museum to house the object on the understanding that it will be gifted at some time in the future/upon their death. Other donors might offer an object with the condition that it is always on display or used and displayed in a certain way or with specific interpretation. It is rare for an object to be accepted by a museum with such conditions as these can often be highly problematic. Only in exceptional circumstances, and after much consultation with curatorial and management staff, may such arrangements be accepted, usually for outstanding objects and with a written contract.

Staff can sometimes be asked to provide financial appraisals of objects before they are offered to the museum. Such a service should not be provided by museums, and this practice is not lawful in the US.[7] Such requests should be politely declined, and the donor should be encouraged to seek advice from professional valuers.

LOANS

The process for considering and rejecting or accepting loans to the museum is similar to that of donations. An offer record should be made (see Offer or potential purchase record below) and if the museum decides to accept the object, details about it should be recorded in the object entry register and loans file, in accordance with museum documentation standards (see Chapter 4, Collections Documentation Policies, Plans and Procedures)

Museums should ensure they follow formal processes when accepting loans.[8] Before a loan is confirmed, agreements should be documented (See Chapter 4, Loans policies). Sometimes loans might be offered to the museum with no set end date; such practices should be avoided as the lender may request the return of their object at any time. Furthermore, if the museum decides it wants to return the object but cannot trace the owner, then it will still need to be accounted for, stored, insured and cared for.

PURCHASES

A museum's Acquisitions Policy should include guidelines for the purchase of objects. It might set out:

- Who is responsible for investigating and approving purchases.
- Acceptable sources of objects/vendors through which to purchase.
- Restrictions on what can be purchased.
- Ethical guidelines the museum should be operating within for acquiring objects.
- The safeguards that should be implemented to ensure the museum buys at a fair price.
- If funding sources for acquisitions should be formally acknowledged through interpretation or publicity material.

A typical process for the purchase of objects will follow that set out above for donations. Consideration may need to be given as to whether fundraising needs to take place in order to raise funds for the purchase, perhaps by approaching donors or through a public appeal.

Offer or potential purchase record

When an object is offered to a museum through donation or loan, or if an object is considered for purchase, the museum should make a record of it, even if it is ultimately not accessioned into the collection. This might be a useful way to trace objects if more information becomes available in the future. Copies of correspondence concerning the object, research undertaken, or minutes of collections development committee meetings should also be retained.

Confirming provenance and ownership

As noted in Chapter 2, museums must operate within certain legal and ethical frameworks when collecting objects, they have an important responsibility when it comes to ascertaining the provenance of items in their collections. Museums should carefully consider whether to collect objects of unclear or questionable authorship; with unproven historical associations; of unverified authorship; that have been collected in ways that caused environmental damage; or are human remains or objects of particular cultural or spiritual significance.[9]

Sometimes an object's early provenance is lost, forgotten, mistaken or even forged and museums must make concerted efforts to confirm previous ownership and trace the origins of objects. The authenticity of objects should also be confirmed as far as possible, in order to prevent fakes and forgeries entering the collections. Museum staff should try to authenticate objects through research and enquiry, and through 'scientific, historical or stylistic analysis'.[10] One way to confirm authenticity of an object is through written records, photographs and oral testimonies: this relies heavily on the survival of good quality and abundant records. Details of an object might also be examined through stylistic analysis, perhaps through the detection of mistakes or inconsistencies or the comparison of objects produced by the same maker, at the same time and in the same style. Finally, scientific examination undertaken by qualified experts might consider the 'physical nature, composition and structure' of an object:[11] These may use non-destructive techniques (for example, visual and microscopic examination, photography, ultraviolet investigation, radiography, reflectography, X-ray) or destructive techniques (the material analysis of minute samples of the object and identification via dendrochronology and paint analysis).

Entry process

When an object formally enters a museum's collection it must be formally recorded, in accordance with the museum's Collections Documentation Policy (see Chapter 4). The object will be assigned an entry number and its details recorded in an Entry Form (or Deposit Form).[12] This procedure should be followed if the object is a confirmed donation, purchase or loan and even if the object is only being accepted temporarily so that its official acquisition can be considered. Intermediate guardianship in this way for long periods should be avoided: such an arrangement may have some complicated implications for insurance and museums may find that donors become uncontactable in future.

Entry Forms should always be completed in accordance with recognised international or national standards.[13] Most museums in the UK follow the Spectrum data standards (for more on this, see Chapter 4, Collections management standards). Details to be captured will include:

- Object entry number.
- Entry date.
- Name, address, phone number and email address of contact, donor or seller.
- Number of objects deposited.
- Brief description of object(s) and associated information (plus photograph if possible).
- Condition of object(s).
- Reason for entry to collection and method of entry (sale, potential or confirmed gift, bequest etc.).
- Any conditions connected to the entry.
- Date object should be returned, or a decision made.
- Signature of depositor and/or owner.
- Name, job title and signature of museum staff member authorised to complete Entry Form.
- Insurance provisions and valuation (if available).
- Notes on storage, packing or display requirements.

For donations and sales this form is an important step in the formal transfer of ownership of the object to the museum, as it contains the signature of the seller or donor. An Entry Form should be completed in triplicate: one copy is retained by the donor or seller, one goes into the museum's object entry file (ordered sequentially), and one copy stays with the object until it is accepted into the collection.

Accessioning

Following entry to the museum (acquisition), an object may or may not formally (and legally) become part of the collection through a process known as accessioning (for object exit at this point, see below, Exit process). When an object is accessioned it formally enters the collections (in theory, in perpetuity) and its ownership is transferred to the museum.[14] The term 'Title' is used to describe the legal right to possess an object, and a museum will require documentation that shows they hold the title to an object (for example, a receipt, a collecting permit or an import declaration, transfer of copyright).[15]

When a museum decides to formally accession an object into the collection an additional form should be completed, known as the Transfer of Title Form (or Donation Form).[16] This form is the final way a museum can prove its legal ownership of an object. Upon accession into the collections an object must be assigned a unique accession number and its details entered into the museum's accessions register. This working book or file (numbered sequentially) should record specific details about the objects, their history/provenance, and accession numbers when they enter the collections.[17] If the accessions register is a physical book or file it must be kept safely and securely, ideally in a fireproof location.[18]

Accepted practice for accession numbers is to use a two-part system: the year of accession and the next number in the accessions register (for example, 2019.57 is the 57th object to be acquired in 2019). It is possible to assign one number to a group of objects and use a third number to identify these parts (for example, 2019.57.17 is the 17th item in the 57th acquisition of 2019). This is a useful system if it seems appropriate or useful to group certain objects together, for example, in the case of a tea set, or a sketchbook containing many individual drawings. The accession number is a way of identifying the object and linking it to all the data a museum holds on it. This accession number will be permanently associated with the object and should be marked on it in some way if appropriate: the method of marking must be chosen through consultation with a conservator. Upon accession into the collection a new record should be created for the object on the museum's cataloguing system, and all information known about the object recorded here. If funds are available, the object should also be photographed, and the images added to the catalogue and object file.

Collecting information

More data should be added to an object's catalogue entry and object file as more research is carried out, or more information becomes available (see Chapter 4, Collections documentation). If sufficient data about an object is not collected at the time of its entry into the collection, and this information is not added to over time, then the object may be of limited use and significance to the museum.[19] A curator should prepare a list of questions to ask about an object when it is acquired by the museum (usually directed at the donor or seller). These may include:

- Object name: What do they call the object? Is it/has it ever been called anything else? What was its original name?
- Materials: What is the object made from? What are the origins of the materials? Where were these materials obtained?
- Making: When and where was it made? Who was it made by? Are there any details known about the maker? Did they make other things like this? Why was it made? How was it made, and with what? Was it made for someone or somewhere in particular?
- History: Where was it originally kept or used? How many other owners did it have? Is anything known about who they were/are? How was it transferred between owners?
- Use: What was the original use of the object? What is the purpose of the object? Has this changed over time? Who used it? When was it used and how often? Where is it kept now and how?
- Association: Is the object associated with any stylistic terms? Does the object have connections to any groups or individuals not already discussed?
- Physical state: Is the object damaged in any way? Has the object ever been altered? Are any parts of the object decaying or missing? Does the object have any inscriptions or identifying marks?

- Documentation: Are there any documents connected with the object, its maker or former owners (for example, letters, receipts, diaries, ledgers, accounts)? Any photographs or drawings? This will extend to documents relating to the legal status of the object, for example, receipts, invoices, collecting permits, custom forms, letters from the donor, deed of gift etc.
- Details of the donor or seller: If possible, their name, address, telephone number and email address should be recorded. They should be asked if their data can be kept and if they might be contacted by the museum in future. How did they acquire the object? Why did they want to own it? Do they have any relationship with the maker or the previous owners?

Exit process

Objects will not just enter but may also leave a museum's collection for a variety of reasons. Loans in will be returned, loans out will be made, and objects rejected for permanent entry to the collection will be returned to their donors. In all cases the object exit and loans out procedures of the museum should be followed (see Chapter 4, Collections documentation policies, plans and procedures). In the case of loans, museums should ensure objects are issued and returned in accordance with the terms of the loan agreement. Whenever an object leaves the collection an object Exit Form should be completed capturing:

- Object entry number or accession number.
- Name, job title and signature of museum staff member authorising exit.
- Brief description of object and associated information.
- Condition of object.
- Reason for exit and method of delivery.
- Name, address, phone number and email address of person removing or receiving object.
- Date of exit of object and delivery to recipient.
- Any conditions connected to exit.
- Date object should be returned to museum (if a loan out).

- Insurance provisions and valuation (if needed).
- Notes on storage, packing or display requirements.[20]

An Exit Form should be completed in triplicate: once copy is to be retained by the person removing or receiving the object, one is placed in the museum's object exit file (ordered sequentially), and one copy added to the object file or loans file.[21]

Deaccessions policies

Why museums may choose to deaccession objects from their collections has been discussed in Chapter 2, Collections rationalisation, and museums must devise a Deaccessions Policy as part of their Collections Development Policy. The policy might include the following detail:

- How objects considered for disposal should be formally and carefully reviewed with reference to the museum's collecting priorities and plans, current and future resources.
- If an object should be part of the museum's collection for a certain period before being considered for deaccession.
- What consultation, discussion and level of authorisation will be required to authorise a deaccession.
- Which external stakeholders and consultants should be involved in the decision-making process and how their views should be taken into account.
- What processes should be followed in the event of an object being considered for deaccession having unclear or disputed ownership.
- How the museum might consider whether the object could stay in the museum to be used in another capacity (for example, in a handling collection or as 'set dressing').
- If any person who contributed to the donation, purchase or restoration of an object should be consulted before deaccessioning occurs (for example, the original donor).
- The records of the decision-making process, deaccessioning and disposal process that should be kept.

- Suggestions for how, in the first instance, the object could be offered to another (accredited) museum (for example, as a gift, exchange or purchase).
- What any proceeds of sale should be used for.
- The museum's policy on the sale or gift of objects to the staff or members of the governing body of the museum, their families or close friends.
- How objects that have been proven to be fakes or forgeries should be permanently marked as such.
- When objects might be destroyed (for example, only in extreme cases and if after consultation with a conservator).

4

Classifying, recording and cataloguing objects

Collections management

A collection is a museum's most valuable resource, acting as the foundation for the many activities it undertakes. The professional and expert management and care of collections is therefore central to the success of a museum and without this the power of objects in the museum's collections will be severely limited. This chapter will examine the practices that ensure collection objects are kept in safe environments, are sufficiently and appropriately documented, developed for the future, and available for use.[1] As custodians of collections, curators must have a firm understanding of the principles and practice of collections management and a working knowledge of accepted professional standards.[2]

In the last 25 years, the museums sector has seen a significant expansion in knowledge and expertise, and improvement in standards, of collections management and care. Museum accreditation schemes in many countries now specify baseline standards that organisations must meet in this area.[3] A museum with professional collections management systems shows it is acting responsibly to care for its collections and working to carefully balance the need to preserve objects with the desire for access.[4] Collections management should be holistic, addressing every aspect of the object's life and activity in the museum and ensuring all information and expertise is coordinated and accessible.[5] It should be central to the operations of every museum, and input to the systems, plans and procedures should be sought from across the organisation, from a variety of departments and staff.

Collections management policies

As part of an integrated approach to collections management, museums should devise and implement an overarching core policy statement, known as a Collections Management Policy (CMP).[6] The CMP is a high-level strategy that aims to clarify the role of the museum, its purpose, staff, collections and activities. The CMP will capture why a museum exists at all, what its goals are, how its collections assist in meeting these goals, and the professional standards through which it operates relating to the objects it cares for.[7] It will also ensure that objects in the museum are acquired ethically and legally, and they are 'properly managed, housed, secured, conserved, documented, and used.'[8]

Each CMP will be unique to the museum for which it is made, and the content will be specific to the present mission and future priorities and needs of that museum. The final CMP will contain information on:

- The purpose of the museum and its mission, its core aims and objectives.
- Aspects that make the museum special and unique, and a vision for how it will sustain itself in the future.
- The present scope of the museum's collections and how they are employed to achieve the museum's mission and overall aims.
- How the museum's collections are currently managed (for example, by which boards, committees and staff).
- Who the museum's audiences are, what they want, and how their needs are (and could be better) served by the collections.
- The museum's Collections Development Policy (to include the museum's Acquisitions and Deaccessions Policy).

- The museum's Collections Documentation Policy (also known as the Collections Information Policy).
- The museum's Collections Documentation Plan and Documentation Procedures.
- The museum's Collections Care and Conservation Policy (to include security and insurance provision and procedures for the collections, and the Emergency or Disaster Plan).
- The museum's Collections Care and Conservation Plan.
- The museum's vision for access to collections and connections to its users, to include an Access Policy, Access Plan and Procedures.
- The museum's Security Policy, Plan and Procedures.[9]

The CMP should recognise and connect to relevant legal and statutory requirements relating to the museums operations and the care and management of its collections.[10] The policy should also consider the ethical guidelines that the museum must operate within.[11] Composing a CMP is a complex and lengthy task that requires significant reflection, consultation and input from many different stakeholders. The policy should go through multiple stages of review and adjustment, until it is finally approved by the museum's governing body and formally implemented. The CMP should act as a guide for the museum's staff in collections stewardship and be made available to the public in order for the museum to show transparency.[12] The policy should be kept up to date and periodically (and seriously) reviewed every three to five years.

Policies, plans and procedures

As noted above, a museum's CMP will contain certain plans, policies and procedures. Policies are the guidelines and directions set by the museum, they may explain what needs to be done, the principles behind something, and the rules by which decisions and outcomes should be managed. Within the CMP there will be:

- The Collections Development Policy (see Chapter 2).
- The Documentation Policy (or Collections Information Policy, discussed later in this chapter).
- The Care and Conservation Policy (see Chapter 5).

- The Collections Access Policy (discussed later in this chapter).
- The Loans Policy (discussed later in this chapter).

These policies provide clear guidance and strategy in defined areas and each policy must include details of staff responsibility and state who has the authority to make decisions in each area.

Plans set out objectives and detail the vision and ways through which these objectives will be achieved (for example, what needs to be done, when, by who, and how).[13] Plans in a CMP will help the museum to achieve its purpose and mission, these include:

- The Documentation Plan (discussed later in this chapter).
- The Care and Conservation Plan (see Chapter 5).
- The Access Plan (see below and Chapter 8).

Procedures set out the way things will be done, for example, the practical management of collections, and implementation of the policies. Operating according to clear procedures ensures consistency, in the CMP these will include:

- Documentation procedures (discussed later in this chapter).
- Procedures stating how objects should be stored and displayed, moved, marked and conserved (see Chapter 5).
- Procedures exploring how the museum will enable access to the collections.

Collections management standards

Museum registration is an umbrella term for many different activities within the museum, including object entry, acquisition and disposal, documentation, location control, loans management and insurance administration. There is no standard for museum registration: procedures and requirements vary from country to country.[14] Many museums recognise and employ the Spectrum standard in their collections management policies and procedures: this detailed framework is recognised internationally as the 'industry standard' for the management of museum objects and is used in over 100 countries around the world.[15]

The standard is broken down into a series of 21 individual procedures, each describing how objects should be managed and information recorded. Some of these procedures are common activities that happen daily (for example, cataloguing objects), other procedures are more specific and only carried out on occasion (for example, deaccessioning objects). There are 9 primary procedures (ones that museums will use most of the time):

1 Object entry.
2 Acquisition and accessioning.
3 Location and movement control.
4 Inventory.
5 Cataloguing.
6 Object exit.
7 Loans in (borrowing objects).
8 Loans out (lending objects).
9 Documentation planning.[16]

There are also 12 'non-primary procedures'. These will be used more occasionally in museum work, but it is still essential that a museum shows it is aware of the procedures and has clearly defined policies in these areas:

1 Condition checking and technical assessment.
2 Collections care and conservation.
3 Valuation.
4 Insurance and indemnity.
5 Emergency planning for collections.
6 Damage and loss.
7 Deaccessioning and disposal.
8 Rights management.
9 Reproduction.
10 Use of collections.
11 Collection review.
12 Audit.[17]

Collections documentation

ICOM's *Code of Ethics for Museums* is clear on the need for museums to adequately record information about collections, and to maintain high standards in this documentation and data management (see section 2.18 and 2.20).[18] The adequate and appropriate documentation of collections also forms a key part of many of the primary Spectrum procedures. Museums should have established systems that will enable them to capture all the information relating to an object, its biography and importance, accurately and permanently.[19] Recording adequate information about an object will help to establish the legal status of an object within the museum (or one that is on loan to the museum), and will ensure the museum can properly account for its objects by recording their movement and condition. Ensuring this documentation is detailed, accurate and accessible will enable the object to be used to its fullest in the research, exhibition, outreach and education work of the museum.[20] An absence of official records can also hinder efforts to take appropriate action in the case of suspected theft or illicit trafficking of objects.[21]

At least one member of staff in any museum should be assigned responsibility for overseeing and monitoring collections documentation activity. In small museums this duty may fall to a curator. In larger organisations it might be possible (and necessary) to appoint a registrar to head up all activity in this area.[22]

Object biographies

Almost every object that enters a museum collection will have a story connected to it, and new stories will be created for that object once it is in the museum. It is important to adequately record these stories in a timely fashion[23]. When museums consider what to document about an object it is often useful to think of it in terms of creating a biography. This might include details of who made it, who owned it, how, when and where it has been used and by whom. Such biographical information can help museums tell stories about objects; assign value and meaning to them; relate objects to one another; tell wider stories about groups of objects; and help visitors understand them more fully or appreciate and relate to them more deeply.[24]

Collections documentation policies, plans and procedures

Within a Collections Management Policy will be a Collections Documentation Policy statement, which details the museum's intentions to gather, record and store information about its collections, and make this accessible and/or actively share it.[25] The Documentation Policy will ensure that information on the museum's collections and the procedures surrounding documentation are managed professionally and that the information relating to collection objects can be accessed by a range of users. The Documentation Policy will outline what types of records the museum will keep (for example, records relating to object entry, ownership, movement, marking and labelling, conservation, exhibition, loans), what information will be recorded, and who is responsible for making and maintaining the records. The policy might set out a museum's commitment to improving its systems and what standards it aims to achieve. Curatorial staff should periodically review the museum's documentation of collection objects to check that it meets the minimum standards expected and agreed in its policies. A Collections Documentation Plan will address the steps the museum will take to remedy any backlog it may have in documenting and recording its collections (retrospective documentation and cataloguing).[26]

Documentation procedures for collections within a museum should be set out in a documentation procedural manual. This should act as a reference document for staff in the museum and ensure collections documentation is undertaken to agreed consistent standards. The manual should state who has responsibility for overseeing the museum's documentation procedures; which staff should undertake the work (and who has authorisation to do so); at what stage; and timeframes for when the work should be undertaken and completed. The manual should also include detailed instructions for the use of an electronic database to record information about an object, standards for uploading images and guidance on retrieving records and information.

Collections management systems

A museum's Collections Management System (also known as CMS) is the means through which individual objects in the collection can be identified and tracked and all information known about them sufficiently recorded, managed and accessed. It also enables easy cross-referencing with other information sources in the museum relating to an object.[27] In the past this was done through the use of paper records, kept in numerical order (by accession number) in a card cabinet (ideally fireproof and lockable). Today, it is more common for museums to use a computer database for this work and to digitise or photograph the paper-based records and add the information to the system.[28]

A digital CMS should provide for easy retrieval of object information and must be able to accommodate rapidly expanding numbers of different types of object records.[29] It should enable the recording of prior ownership and all activity connected to the object (for example, loans, exhibitions, conservation work).[30] The system should not limit the total possible size of any record and should allow for cross-referencing between the different types of information recorded about each object. It is also essential for a CMS to have a secure and fail-safe backup system.

Each museum will choose its own Collections Management System. It is possible to develop in-house database systems, but these often require a great deal of staff time, energy and expertise to develop and maintain. Commercially available systems can be more reliable and functional: several companies design 'off-the-shelf' cataloguing systems specifically for museums and there is a wide range to choose from. Alternatively, a museum can choose to work with a specialist company to modify an existing CMS programme and tailor it more closely to their requirements as well as pay a subscription to receive ongoing support.

Classification of objects

Cataloguing an object will provide the museum with an opportunity to classify it. This might be according to certain criteria, subjects or areas of interest. When objects are assigned certain keyword terms in their electronic records searches can be made to generate groups of objects with certain similar characteristics (for example, of the same type, medium, artist, subject, date, given by the same donor, or stored in the same place etc.). Different museums will choose to classify their objects using different typologies.[31]

A common challenge in the practice of classifying objects by entering data about them in a catalogue is the control of terminology. If subjects, names or locations have been entered in a variety of ways and formats by museum staff then it will be very difficult, and often impossible, to create comprehensive and accurate lists using certain criteria.[32] For example, the 19th-century French painter Claude Oscar Monet might be recorded by one member of staff for one object as 'C. O. Monet', then by another for a different object as 'Claude Monet' and still another as 'C. Monet'. Thus, searching for all objects in the collection by entering the term 'Claude Oscar Monet' may not produce a list containing all the objects in the collection associated with the artist. One way to overcome this problem is to standardise the terms used when cataloguing objects to ensure consistency.[33] This can be done in any field (object name, subject, materials, location etc.). In many electronic cataloguing systems, it is possible to create predefined fields in which only one possible form of a term, name or place can be selected from a drop-down menu.

Indexing systems enable objects to be found easily, and particular groups to be retrieved. A wide range of indexes can be generated on an electronic database to match with the exact type of objects in the collection or specific requirements of the museum (for example, through things like object name, subject, style, period, marker, location). Each museum must decide which terms are most often used, or groups of objects are most frequently requested. It is also possible to implement a hierarchical structure within a catalogue to enable the objects to be classified according to the narrowest possible category. For example, within the category 'footwear' might be 'shoe' and 'boot', and further within 'boot' might be 'wellington boot', 'riding boot', 'walking boot', etc. There are pre-prepared terminology packages available that can be added to catalogues, developed by specialist groups.

Movement control

A Collections Management System should have provision for the recording of the location of an object in the museum. It is essential to record the movement of objects both outside of and within the museum to prevent an object being lost. Each time an object is moved, a note must be made in the museum's CMS to record the date the object was moved, by whom, why and where, even if this is a temporary and/or short-term move.[34] Guidance notes might be added to the catalogue record if there are restrictions on how, when and where an object can be moved.

Loans policies

As noted in Chapter 2, How museums collect, museums often consider loaning their objects to other organisations for a specified length of time, and frequently borrow objects on a short-term basis. Composing a Loans Policy enables a museum to clearly state what and when they will loan and borrow, and to or from whom.

A Loans Out Policy might state:

- To which organisations loans may be made.
- What objects can be lent and for what purpose.
- For how long loans may be made (always for a finite period), if renewal is possible, and the procedures for recalling a loan.
- If costs of the loan should be covered in full by the borrowing institution and if any fees will be charged.
- The process through which applications for loans should be made, processed and documented.
- How loans will be considered and approved (including procedures for resolving any concerns regarding travel, environment, display).
- What insurance will be required, and which party is responsible for providing it (typically the borrowing institution).
- How and when a condition report should be commissioned.
- The facilities reports required from the borrowing institution (display and storage conditions and monitoring, security and disaster planning provisions).
- Any restrictions on loans (for example, photography of the object(s), use of images by the borrowers in publicity, reproductions and alterations to objects).

A museum should also devise a Loans In Policy, this should outline:

- What objects might be borrowed by the museum, and why (linking to the museum's mission).
- Who the museum should borrow from.
- If the museum should borrow objects if there are any issues or problems with their transport, condition, display or storage.

- The process for approving loans (including the review of any restrictions on the loan).
- The process for ensuring any conditions of loan are met, and how facilities reports should be arranged and issued.
- How the value of the object should be determined and how objects will be insured.
- The procedures to be followed and documentation required for proposing, approving and processing a loan.

In addition to these documents, when an object is loaned to another organisation a museum will create a loan agreement, containing the following information:

- Names and contact details of the parties involved in the loan.
- Which objects are being loaned and the purpose of the loan.
- The start and end date of the loan.
- Any restrictions on the loan (for example, if the object can be photographed).
- Conditions under which the contract can be modified (for example, early return of the object or extension of the loan term).
- How the objects should be cared for, displayed, stored, packaged and transported.

Access policies, plans and procedures

Providing access to collections and information for a wide range of users is an important aspect of museum work. An Access Policy should consider how the museum:

- Is meeting the legal requirements relating to access (for example, national legislation surrounding disability and discrimination) and already providing access for all users.
- Is evaluating its operations and outlook in order to provide access to collections, ideas and facilities to as wide a range of people as possible (so not just physical, but also intellectual access).

- Is taking steps to engage with current and potential new visitors to find out their needs and interests, and to identify barriers to access and participation.

Access Plans will set out the museum's strategy for addressing any weaknesses in its access provisions. The plan will set out what needs to be done, the priorities for the actions, the resources available, who will be responsible for the actions, and over what timeframe. Finally, Access Procedures set out what procedures should be followed in order to enable access to collections through research, public enquiries, photography, learning events and other activities.[35] This subject is explored in further detail in Chapter 8, Access policies and plans.

5 Handling, storing and preserving objects

This book began by questioning what a museum is. Definitions of the term museum usually suggest they are organisations that acquire and preserve objects (or in the case of the ICOM definition, acquire and preserve 'heritage').[1] Indeed, we might question whether a museum without objects can exist at all, because so many museum activities and functions rely on the existence of a collection.[2] Consciously collecting objects would make no sense if these objects were allowed to decay. Caring for objects so that they do not become damaged or disappear is therefore essential to the work of a museum and this chapter provides an overview of the main aspects of this work.

Collections care and conservation in museums is a broad subject, and includes aspects such as display and storage conditions, handling packing and transport, condition reporting, risk assessments, security, insurance, disaster management, preventative conservation, reactive/remedial conservation and restoration.[3] Collections care should be woven into a museum's mission statement and embedded in the organisation's objectives.[4]

Collections care and conservation policies and plans

Chapter 4 discussed the need for a museum to devise and implement a Collections Management Policy (CMP). Within this must be a Collections Care and Conservation Policy, an approved statement outlining the museum's long-term approach and commitment to the care and conservation of its collections. The policy should outline the national and international legal and ethical guidelines, principles and sector standards the museum will follow and what measures it will take to ensure the long-term preservation of its collections. The policy should also show the museum's commitment to obtaining expert advice, guidance and services in collections conservation and security matters.

Within the CMP will also be a Collections Care and Conservation Plan, setting out the museum's objectives and planned actions needed to maintain and/or improve standards of collections care and conservation. This plan must be informed by data gathered from audits of the museum's current collections care provisions; reviews of any building maintenance programmes; assessments of current display and storage conditions; examinations of data collected through environmental monitoring; and advice from professional conservators or other experts.

The Collections Care and Conservation Policy and Collections Care and Conservation Plan are wide-ranging documents, covering details of:

- Current storage and display facilities and conditions (and plans for managing future).
- Conservation risk assessments and auditing plans and procedures.
- Staff members responsible for certain aspects of the policy.
- The role of conservators (guidance and services currently sought and provided).
- The inspection and maintenance programme for preventative and remedial works.
- The monitoring and maintenance of conditions in storage and display areas.
- The housekeeping plan and manual of procedures.
- The Integrated Pest Management Plan.
- The documentation of conservation matters (for example, condition reports, environmental monitoring records, building maintenance records).

- Condition checking of objects: when it will be undertaken and how reports should be produced.
- The handling policy for collection objects, including who is authorised to handle objects and what training will be provided.
- Guidelines for packing and storing objects.
- Appropriate materials and methods to be used in storage and display of objects.
- The loan of objects and the policy as regards transport, handling, packing, environmental conditions, and insurance.
- The remedial conservation programme for collection objects.
- The plans and procedures for regular inventorying of the collection.
- The security and insurance provisions and procedures.
- The emergency plan and disaster plan.[5]

Preventative conservation

In a museum, conservation policies and procedures should focus primarily on detecting potential agents of deterioration and mitigating, or entirely preventing, their effects on museum objects. All aspects of the ways a museum handles, maintains, stores, displays and transports objects should be carefully controlled so that they do not become damaged (or further damaged), and if they do decay, they do so at the slowest possible rate.[6]

An approach to conservation that is preventative, rather than reactionary, should be a priority for any museum because it can save a great deal of time, effort and financial resources in the long term. It can also mean that museum objects survive into the future, when they may not otherwise have done, and reduce the need to carry out remedial conservation.[7] Preventative conservation work needs to be carried out on a near daily basis, rather than every now and then or in reaction to problems that could have been prevented. Curators and conservators may need to campaign for the investment of time and money for new equipment, infrastructure and staff, using their knowledge and existing evidence to persuade museum managers that the initial costs could be offset by reductions in the costs of remedial conservation and the long-term survival of the collections.[8]

Preventative conservation: basic principles

The following guidelines should be followed when adopting a preventative conservation approach:

- Ensure all staff have at least a basic understanding of the benefits and practice of preventative conservation.
- Handle objects with proper care and with regard to their particular nature.
- Provide formal training for staff who work directly with the collection.
- Do not eat, drink or smoke anywhere near collection objects.
- Ensure that relative humidity and temperature are kept at stable and appropriate levels in storage and display areas.
- Ensure light levels are appropriate for the objects on display.
- Monitor environmental conditions regularly and keep records.
- Ensure materials used in storage and display are not harmful to the objects.
- Maintain equipment and environmental control systems regularly.
- Check collections regularly for signs of pest infestation.
- Keep storage areas tidy and clean.
- Provide sufficient space in storage areas and containers (avoid crushing or stacking objects) and allow for air flow and ventilation.
- Keep objects away from external walls and off floors if dampness or flooding is likely.
- Avoid excessive cleaning, the use of significant amount of water, or domestic/regular cleaning agents in display and storage areas.
- Only carry out cleaning of objects following expert advice.[9]

Environmental conditions

Maintaining stable storage and display environments (for example, relative humidity, temperature and light levels) will assist in minimising further damage or deterioration to museum objects.[10] Different objects made of different materials will have slightly different requirements in these areas and optimal storage and display conditions therefore vary.

LIGHT

To a greater or lesser extent, all objects are affected by light, but some materials are particularly sensitive, and light can cause significant damage or pose a serious threat to their survival; natural light is particularly destructive.[11] The intensity of light can be measured in units of *lux*, using a light meter. Light levels should be recorded regularly so that analysis of data over time is possible. Regulating levels of daylight is difficult, which is why some museums eliminate it entirely and rely on artificial sources. In general, museum objects should only be exposed to light in the range 50–200 *lux*.[12] Levels for oil/tempera paintings, wood, bone, stone and ivory should not exceed 200 *lux*. Ideally, watercolours, prints and drawings, manuscripts, textiles, costume, natural history and ethnographic objects should only be illuminated by light of up to 50 *lux*. Ultraviolet (UV) radiation is particularly damaging and should be kept below 75 microwatts per lumen (*uw/lmi*), measured using a UV monitor.

These levels are the ideal, and not always possible. Individual museums should consider the full range of possibilities, restrictions, implications and the benefits to both the objects and visitors of adopting these levels. Today, many museums set display limitations according to annual exposure limits, so enabling more light to fall on an object than noted, but for shorter periods of time.[13] It is impossible to eliminate all light from storage and display areas, but the time that objects are exposed to light and the intensity of that light can be reduced and controlled through the following approaches:

- Not allowing daylight to fall directly on objects.
- Blacking out windows and relying on artificial lighting.
- Reducing the number and wattage of lights.
- Using LED lights (importantly lights that do not emit heat).
- Fitting lights on the outside (not inside) of display cases.
- Using dimmer switches.
- Installing motion sensors or putting lights on timers.
- Using screens or covers that can be lifted by visitors.
- Using curtains, blinds or shutters on windows when the museum is closed.
- Installing semi-transparent blinds.
- Installing UV film on windows and display cases.
- Installing low levels of lighting in storage spaces.

HUMIDITY AND TEMPEATURE

Relative humidity (RH) can be measured with a hygrometer. The levels are expressed as a percentage: the ratio of water vapour in the air compared to the amount it could hold if fully saturated. Low percentage values indicate dry conditions and high values suggest the air is already very humid (for example, in wet weather). In the first instance museums should try to eliminate extremes in RH and temperature, and control sudden changes or regular fluctuations in levels as a result of seasonal changes. Extreme levels and/or large fluctuations will cause the materials from which objects are made to contract, expand, dry out and/or oxidise, so damage is likely to result. In very humid conditions condensation, mould and fungus might also affect the objects. Ideal RH levels should be around 50–55 per cent RH for a mixed collection.[14] Extremes of above 60 per cent RH and below 40 per cent RH should be avoided.

Museum collections should not be kept under conditions of extreme heat or cold. An ideal temperature for a mixed collection is 18–20°C. Storage spaces might be kept at a slightly lower level, perhaps 15°C. Where stores are also used by staff as working spaces the need for slightly higher temperatures should be considered, and comfort heating systems installed. Changes in temperature in display and storage spaces may also affect levels of RH: the ability of the air to hold water vapour increases at higher temperatures and decreases at lower temperatures. It is sometimes possible to control temperature and humidity levels simply by using the museum's existing heating system, but often additional humidifiers and dehumidifiers need to be introduced. If desired, a full air conditioning system (perhaps with thermostats for different areas of the museum) might be installed.

DUST, DIRT AND AIR POLLUTION

Museum spaces in which staff work and visitors gather will always accumulate dust, dirt, minute inorganic and organic particles of grit, soot, environmental pollutants, skin, textiles, plant fibres, pollen, pests and general everyday debris.[15] These can work as agents of deterioration and it is important to control these factors in museum spaces. Dust and dirt can settle on museum objects; this can look unsightly and cause serious damage to them in the long term (corrosion, mould growth, compacted and cemented dust).[16] Dust and dirt might be cleaned off museum objects, but this should only be carried out by appropriately trained specialists. Preventing dust and dirt from reaching the objects in the first place is a better approach and can be achieved through a rigorous and sustained housekeeping regime:

- Cleaning all gallery and storage areas thoroughly and frequently, using a specialist museum-grade vacuum cleaner.
- Using good-quality display cases that are resistant to dust.
- Periodically cleaning surfaces and interiors of display cases/ shelves/plinths/floors (decanting objects first).
- Shutting and sealing windows and doors not in use.
- Ensuring large objects are fitted with dust covers when in storage.
- Installing an air conditioning or air filtering system.
- Controlling the consumption of food in gallery spaces.

PESTS

Museums are highly likely to attract insects and rodents. These animals can cause a great deal of short- and long-term damage to collection objects. Museums should devise and implement an Integrated Pest Management Plan: this is a multi-layered, proactive approach to collections care, which attempts to prevent any infestation in the museum in the first place and to use natural approaches and materials to remove any pests without affecting the environment.[17] Regular inspection in order to detect pests, assess the extent of the problem, and devise plans to prevent them from reaching collection objects and eliminate them from the museum is key.

Environmental control is important in preventing a pest infestation: temperatures of over 20°C can encourage pests, as can warm, damp and cluttered spaces with high humidity. Ideally display cases should be of sufficient quality and prohibit the entry of pests.[18] Good housekeeping is also essential and all areas of the museum should be regularly vacuumed to remove organic debris.[19] A museum should implement a food and drink policy and ensure that these items are not consumed in galleries and stores: the uncontrolled presence of food and drink in museum spaces greatly increases the likelihood of a pest infestation.[20] Some museums may install traps, to try and reduce or to monitor the numbers of pests. Many different types of trap are available, and the type selected should match the pest in question.[21] It is essential to check and refresh the traps at suitable intervals and to thoroughly document whatever is found, in order to consider a suitable solution to the problem.[22]

If an infestation is allowed to take hold then specialist advice from a conservator (and possibly an external specialist pest control company) should be sought. Any methods employed to tackle the problem should be safe and appropriate (fumigation, for example, can be extremely harmful to museum objects and should be avoided). Remedial action should only be undertaken after consultation with a specialist conservator.[23] Possible actions include the removal, quarantining and disposal of infected objects; subjecting objects to extremely low or high temperatures; the use of various controlled atmosphere treatments; the use of insect growth regulators; and the use of pesticide treatment or fumigation (only in very extreme cases and as a last resort).[24]

Environmental monitoring and control

In order to devise and implement a programme of environmental control, museums should carry out surveys to measure, record and analyse information on light, RH and temperature levels and air quality in galleries and storage spaces over the course of a year.[25] Electronic measuring devices can be linked to monitoring software so that the data can be analysed.[26] Not all museums have the resources to implement large-scale changes to the temperature, RH and light levels across their entire premises.[27] It may be impossible to overcome some challenges: for example, regulating the temperature and humidity of historic buildings or eliminating the effects of extreme weather conditions. It is important that every museum assess what level of environmental control is possible and most appropriate with reference to the needs of the particular objects in its collection; the available resources; strength of influence of external factors (for example, climate); and building structure and/or age.[28] It might also be important to consider if any measures the museum implements to control storage and display environments run contrary to other policies (for example, if an air conditioning system compromises the museum's policies in environmental sustainability).[29]

Approved materials and cleaning substances

Certain materials and equipment commonly used to clean domestic and commercial spaces can cause physical and/or chemical damage to museum objects.[30] Ordinary cleaning agents and equipment are not usually suitable for use in museums and alternative products should always be sourced (for example, natural products like vinegar and baking soda; special non-toxic conservation-grade detergents, cleaning agents and waxes; smooth and lint-free sponges; cloths and brushes; and specialist vacuum cleaner attachments). Similarly, certain materials used in the display and storage of objects (for example, wood, fabrics, paints, adhesive tape, plastics, plasticine, rubber, metal pins, wire and hangers) can release compounds in the form of vapour over time that cause them damage. Ideally, all materials used in the display or storage of objects should be inert, tested and certified as suitable for use in museums.

Handling, packing and transportation of objects

Damage to museum objects is most likely to happen during movement and transportation.[31] Sometimes these objects are unique, the only surviving examples of their type, or are noteworthy and special in some way: carefully controlling and having appropriate procedures and training in place relating to the handling, packing and transport of objects, is therefore essential.[32] Museum objects will need to be handled and moved for a variety of reasons but they should only be handled when necessary, and by those who have sufficient knowledge and training to do so following best practice and using suitable equipment.[33] Most museums abide by written procedures, and some of the most important considerations are set out here:[34]

- Be familiar with the health and safety legislation affecting your workplace and your work.
- Ensure any documentation procedures for movement control are carried out before and after the activity.
- Do not let untrained people handle objects without supervision.
- Understand the specific needs of different types of object before handling and moving.
- Examine/inspect the object before picking it up and assess its suitability for handling and movement.
- Have a plan before you start: know where you are going with the object, where you will set it down, and what you will do with it.
- Remove any hanging jewellery or lanyards.

- Wash your hands before and after handling.
- Use appropriate gloves and other protective equipment.
- Concentrate when handling and moving the object, do not do two things at once.
- Always use two hands if possible and support the weight carefully.
- Only carry one object, tray or box at one time.
- Provide cushioning under the object.
- Do not lift objects from weak points (for example, rims, handles).
- Do not slide or drag objects.
- Do not reach across objects or move one object across another.
- Do not pile objects up on top of one another.
- Use suitable moving equipment (for example, trays, trollies, foam).
- Do not overload storage boxes or containers: there should be sufficient space between each object.
- Carefully protect objects with padding and cushioning made of inert and acid-free materials.
- If necessary, apply labels to containers indicating they are fragile.
- Ensure the destination for the object is clean and uncluttered and light levels are appropriate.
- If moving the object, know your route and perhaps ask someone else to supervise and assist (for example, by opening doors, warning others to move out of the way).
- Move at a slow pace and never backwards.
- Use pencil, not ink, when making notes.
- Do not eat, drink, smoke or vape near collection objects.
- If the objects are too large, heavy or fragile seek assistance from specialist museum handlers and transport companies.

PROTECTIVE EQUIPMENT

Secretions from skin can react with some materials and cause damage to museum objects over time. Gloves should be worn when handling most objects in order to protect them and the person handling them (the surface of objects might also have toxic properties). The type of glove to wear will depend on the type of object being handled.[35]

- Cotton gloves for clean and dry objects. Cotton gloves might be washed and reused when they become dirty. These gloves can be too thick and do not offer complete protection from oils from the skin, they may also catch on rough surfaces.

- Disposable vinyl or nitrile gloves for objects that are dirty or very dusty, that have a rough surface or very smooth surface. Many museums reply entirely on disposable nitrile gloves: these are convenient but can often be expensive and cannot be reused.
- Sometimes it is appropriate not to use gloves at all. Clean and dry bare hands might be preferable when handling rare books; fragile paper; oily, smooth, slippery or heavy object; objects that are flaking or very rough; or that might be damaged if gloves are used.

Depending on the work being performed and the objects involved, it will sometimes be necessary to wear Personal Protective Equipment.[36] This might include a lab coat or protective apron, eye goggles, face shields, or a dust mask. Hard hats and steel toe-capped safety boots might be required for very large and heavy objects.

Storage of objects

Most museums will need to keep a proportion of collection objects in store. Ideally, storage spaces should be tailored to their function and the same standards of care must be applied as for display areas.[37] Increasingly, museums are considering the creation of off-site facilities in which collections can be stored under optimal conditions and conservation work can be undertaken.[38] Some museums will have strategies in place to ensure that their stored objects are used and accessed in 'open' or 'accessible' stores (see Chapter 6).[39] When storing objects it is important to:

- House them in a secure and suitable building (might be a custom-built or an adapted space).
- Implement procedures for logging staff and visitors in and out of the space.
- Provide enough space for the movement of objects and people.
- Install cupboards, shelves and racking of adequate size.
- Install moveable shelving to allow for changes in use (free-standing or a roller system).

- Create labels for storage spaces and mark individual sections with lists of items.
- Ensure objects are easy to find and remove.
- Implement procedures and equipment for the safe handling and movement of objects.
- Develop suitable documentation systems and procedures for the entry, location and exit of objects.
- Control and monitor environmental conditions to suit the categories of objects in store.
- Implement regular auditing and stocktaking procedures.
- Undertake regular conservation and security assessments.
- If possible, designate an area for processing, acclimatising and quarantining objects before they enter the main store.
- Store packing and transport crates and materials separately to objects.

Different types of objects may need to be stored in different ways, or under different conditions. It might be possible for museums to group objects made from similar materials and with similar environmental requirements together in separate stores where distinct environmental conditions might be maintained.[40]

Condition reports and inventorying

A condition report is a written record of the physical state of an object, recording in detail any signs of damage, wear or deterioration.[41] Condition reports are useful for ongoing assessment of an object and they become part of the museum's permanent records. Reports should be made when an object first enters the collection.[42] In some museums, resources are available to prepare condition reports periodically for all objects, which are then reissued when the object goes out on display or returns to store. In other museums, condition reports will only be prepared for a limited number of objects (for example, the most valuable, or the most at risk or fragile) or when an object goes out on loan and re-enters the museum.[43] Regular inventories of collections will help to ensure objects are accounted for and provide another opportunity to monitor their condition. The frequency and extent of inventories varies between museums and will depend on the resources available, as well as the potential risks (for example, high-value objects should be checked more frequently).[44]

Remedial conservation

The treatment of a collection object that is already damaged or decayed in order to stabilise it, perhaps 'enhance some aspects of its cultural or scientific value', and to ensure its survival for a longer period of time is known as remedial conservation.[45] The methods of treatment used to clean and remove agents that cause damage should be ones that might be reversed in the future. Remedial conservation can be very costly and time consuming. It is essential to engage a conservator to carry out any remedial conservation work: untrained persons may cause irreversible damage using inappropriate methods and materials. A conservator should work with a curator to identify a programme of remedial conservation and detailed records of the remedial work should be kept.

Restoration

It is important to distinguish between conservation and restoration: while remedial conservation seeks to establish an object's condition and prevent further deterioration, restoration aims to return an object as close to its original state as possible.[46] Substantial cleaning and/or replacing and refreshing significant parts (whether original to the object's manufacture or not) will alter the historical integrity of an object and result in a permanent change, perhaps affecting its historical and aesthetic value. The changes may also cause irreversible damage, immediately or in the future.[47] In museums, restoration is only undertaken after careful consideration of the ethical implications and the likelihood of achieving success. The work should only be carried out if it will enable the object to be used in a particular way that the museum has decided is required, or if the changes will result it being displayed in a more meaningful way.[48] Restoration work should not be undertaken without the involvement and supervision of a trained conservator.[49] Detailed comparative research must be carried out and staff must be able to identify and explain the need for and extent of restoration work on museum objects. Each step of the process must be rigorously documented, and processes must always be reversible.

Working with conservators

Museum conservators are skilled professionals, who have undertaken expert training in the field of collections care and conservation. Their advice, guidance and skills are invaluable to a museum's work in managing and caring for its collections. Many museums do not have the resources to permanently employ an in-house conservation team. Instead, it is common for museums to employ freelance conservators on a contractual basis. With enough education, training and provision of suitable equipment, other museum staff, commonly curators, may carry out certain limited duties relating to collections care and conservation (for example, environmental monitoring, condition and environmental surveys and reports).[50]

A museum should employ expert conservators to:

- Provide guidance and assistance to the museum in composing all aspects of the Collections Care and Conservation Policy and Collections Care and Conservation Plan.
- Provide advice and assistance in implementing environmental monitoring and an Integrated Pest Management Plan.
- Provide training to other museum staff in carrying out environmental monitoring, condition and environmental surveys and reports.
- Carry out assessments and regular audits of the conditions in which objects are displayed and stored and recommend changes.
- Undertake surveys of collection objects, produce condition reports and recommendations for remedial conservation.
- Undertake remedial conservation.
- Assist in the creation of disaster and emergency plans and setting up disaster boxes.

Conservation planning and risk assessment/management

Museums must conscientiously and proactively identify, assess, manage and mitigate any potential risks to collections, facilities and people; resources should be carefully targeted to prevent undesirable changes or impact to the collections and the museum premises.[51] Museums should produce and maintain a risk management policy, covering aspects such as building and maintenance standards and programmes, security provisions, fire detection measures, disaster preparedness, preventative conservation measures and inventorying procedures.[52] The policy should also state who is responsible for devising, implementing and monitoring these policies and procedures. The detail and extent of such a policy will vary from general statements recognising the potential risks and how they might be avoided, to detailed descriptions of how exactly the risks can be eliminated or mitigated.[53]

Collections security

Museums are open to the public and therefore objects are under threat from damage and theft. Security measures, procedures and systems must be in place to protect the museum's buildings, contents, staff and visitors.[54] Preventing loss and damage to collections is one of the priorities for any security policy in a museum.[55] Such an approach will also bolster the museum's reputation as a safe and reliable place for the care of the public's heritage.[56] Placing objects within museum cases that are fixed to floors or walls and robust enough not to be broken or forced open (perhaps with locking and alarm systems) is one way to protect objects. Barriers, ropes and information panels might be used to deter or prevent objects on open display being touched. Framed paintings, prints, and drawings might be screwed to walls and mirror plates might be used.[57] Objects of particularly high value might also be alarmed, and ropes or barriers and cameras installed: a variety of electronic detection systems can be used in museums and the choice of which system to use will depend on the nature of the museum and the collection, and the financial resources available. Security staff are also an essential part of any museum's security system, assisting in deterring criminal or antisocial behaviour and physically responding to any incidents.[58]

Disaster planning

Museums must work to reduce and limit possible damage to collections, buildings and people resulting from natural and man-made disasters (for example, fire, flood, earthquake, tornado, severe storm damage, war damage, explosions, civil unrest, terrorism, vandalism).[59] A museum must devise a formal disaster plan in order to mitigate the effects of disasters and to plan reactions to any incidents.[60] The plan should relate to local or national disaster planning procedures and local and national agencies should be consulted when it is devised. The plan should be reviewed and revised regularly, and staff should be provided with training and practice the procedures at regular intervals.[61] A disaster response team will be formed of key trained individuals who have knowledge of the museum buildings and collections and who can be readily available in the event of a disaster.[62] Disaster control equipment and supplies should always be readily available in the museum (for example, emergency equipment, cleaning and packing supplies, protective clothing, storage containers and damage recording materials).

Insurance of collections

Museums should always be working towards the prevention of loss or damage to objects and premises, however, if loss or damage does happen, compensation may be available.[63] Insurance may provide a level of financial compensation for people and property in the event of certain specified events (loss, theft, destruction, damage, injury) and the details of what is covered should be specified in writing in a formal insurance policy.[64] Insurance approaches and requirements vary from museum to museum and from country to country and specialist insurance companies should be consulted.

The insurance of museum collections is a complicated area, both because collection objects can be so varied and because replacing unique and rare objects is so difficult (often impossible). It is important to have regular valuations of the collections and to update the insurance cover, as prices change frequently.[65] Museums must work with reputable firms and should obtain a quotation for the work before it begins. Unfortunately, not all museums can afford to purchase an insurance policy that covers the full market value of all of their objects.[66] A museum might break down its collections into certain groups, which can then be valued and provided with indemnity insurance.[67] Within these groups might be certain named objects, to be covered individually at an agreed value.[68] Objects on loan from the museum to other organisations will need separate cover, usually provided by the borrower, and if the museum holds any loans these will need to be insured separately.

PART THREE

DISPLAYING AND INTERPRETING COLLECTIONS

6 Displaying objects

The first chapter of this book showed that some of the earliest museums arranged and presented objects in order to enhance understanding of the world. As museums began to open their doors to wider audiences, the function of displaying and exhibiting objects for the education of the public expanded. Most definitions of a museum will consider them as places in which objects are displayed to a public audience, accompanied by messages. In museums, we can have authentic and unique experiences through encountering real objects. Indeed, it is these collections of objects that set museums apart from other organisations and experiences in the cultural, educational and leisure sectors.[1]

When we use the terms 'display' and 'exhibition' in the context of the museum, we are describing a grouping of objects accompanied by interpretive devices (for example, labels, images, video, sound, interactive devices), carefully arranged and considered to communicate and explore certain ideas and subjects. A great deal of thought and effort goes into arranging and bringing meaning to objects in a museum and providing visitors with opportunities to increase their knowledge and understanding, uncover new information and perspectives, and have enjoyable or even transformative experiences.[2]

Public expectations about what museum displays and exhibitions should be, how they should look, and what experiences they should offer, are high, especially if public money has been used to deliver them.[3] Time-constrained audiences, who can also visit theme parks, cinemas, theatres and sports grounds and who use digital technologies daily, demand value for money.[4] Often a museum is judged by the quality of these outputs and a great deal of resources can be devoted to them. It is therefore important that curators are aware of all the considerations, stages and processes surrounding the design and delivery of displays and exhibitions. This chapter provides an overview of this topic.

Permanent displays or temporary exhibitions

Often the words 'display' and 'exhibition' are used interchangeably in the museum sector. In this book a distinction is made between a 'permanent display', and a 'temporary exhibition'. These two types of display usually serve different purposes and are created for different kinds of visitor.[5] In theory, no museums have displays that are completely permanent: this implies that they can remain fixed forever.[6] It is good practice to change a 'permanent' display at least every ten years: ideally, a regular source of funding should be established for the museum's displays to allow for periodic renewals or changes, to avoid the display appearing outdated, tired and containing inaccurate information and antiquated multimedia.[7]

Temporary exhibitions are displays that last for only short-term, temporary periods.[8] They usually have an overarching theme, and can be used to:

- Showcase a new piece of research.
- Examine new subjects (or ones that the museum would not normally examine).
- Commemorate an anniversary.
- Explore new connections and comparisons.
- Consider something exploratory or as a means of provoking debate.

Some temporary exhibitions will be designed to be universally appealing and for a general audience, the theme of others may be directed towards specialist audiences. One major advantage of temporary exhibitions is their ability to attract and encourage visitors who might not otherwise come to the museum, and to potentially raise the profile of the museum.[9] Today the temporary exhibition industry is thriving: most museums recognise the potential benefits and there is an expectation from the public that museums will stage them.[10]

Ideas about what a museum exhibition is have changed: they can now be pop-ups, located in non-traditional spaces, virtual, or travelling. Temporary exhibitions can enable a greater degree of expression and experimentation than is possible in permanent displays. Some might be quickly researched, planned and realised or produced with modest resources, enabling more freedom in content and form. Quite often temporary exhibitions contain heightened elements of 'showmanship', theatricality and perhaps a greater emphasis on providing entertainment or immersing the visitor in an experience.[11]

The inclusion of objects borrowed from other museums, other organisations or from private individuals on a temporary basis is common for museum exhibitions. The loaning and borrowing process should be carefully managed with reference to the museum's Collections Management Policy (see Chapter 4). Some temporary exhibitions can be borrowed in their entirety (including objects, display cases and interpretation, as well as staff to install and de-install them) These are known as travelling exhibitions or circulating shows and might be organised by museums themselves, or by specialist companies.[12]

Reasons for displays

Before planning a display, it is essential to identify the reasons for undertaking the project and the desired result, these might include:[13]

- Refurbishing tired or outdated displays.
- Filling new or empty spaces and/or display cases.
- Expanding the use of collection objects.
- Adding information and knowledge to displays.
- Employing greater use of new research.
- Increasing visitor numbers.
- Diversifying visitor types.[14]

These factors will affect what topics and ideas will be examined in the new display, what objects will be included, how they will be displayed, and the interpretation methods that will be used.

Internal and external collaboration

There is no one way to produce a display or exhibition, organise staff or manage the work. Conceiving of, designing, producing and evaluating museum displays can be a complex and lengthy process.[15] Traditionally, a museum's curator or curatorial team would have researched and organised displays or exhibitions, or at least led the development of the projects. Today, many more staff with expert knowledge and skills will play a part in the process.[16] This will include registrars, conservators, designers, interpretation managers, learning and engagement staff, marketing, PR and social media staff, retail managers, security staff, and perhaps even dedicated exhibition coordinators. These teams will help to deliver displays and exhibitions that are not just based on quality research and interpretation but are also presented in effective ways for maximum impact and include activities and programmes that serve the museum's audiences.[17]

Some museums will work with specialist design and installation companies that can provide expertise a museum may not have in house. These companies work closely with museum staff to produce a final bespoke product that meets the particular requirements of the museum.[18] Some museums will be large enough (and have enough budget) to employ such specialists permanently, potentially supporting an exhibitions (or interpretation) department or members of staff dedicated to coordinating the museum's interpretation, displays and temporary exhibitions programme.[19] Some museums may not have the funds to employ such staff at all, thus the work must necessarily be carried out by an in-house curator with assistance from other colleagues, volunteers and advisors.[20] A third option is for the museum to employ an assistant, guest or exhibition curator on a short-term contract to manage the project. Only sustained and specialist research of a high standard can produce high-quality, successful exhibitions. Not appointing a specialist project curator or allowing an in-house curator enough time to devote to the task is sometimes seen as a cost-saving measure, and is a common challenge for museum staff.

Basic principles for museum displays

Successful museum displays are:

- Attractively designed and visually appealing.
- Entertaining and stimulating.
- Purposeful, with a clear concept and need for the content, with a considered interpretive plan, encouraging visitors to engage with the information and experience.
- Places where information is provided and visitors can explore subjects and ideas at their own pace, in varying degrees of depth according to their interests.
- Well planned, with clear aims and objectives in line with the overall mission and goals of the museum.
- Professionally produced within the available resources and with input from relevant staff and external experts.
- Projects in which the museum building, objects, resources, staff and visitors remain safe and secure.
- Accessible in design and content to as wide a range of users as possible.
- Sensitive and sympathetic to contemporary society, values and attitudes, sometimes encouraging debate and with a critical edge.[21]

Generating concepts for displays and exhibitions

It might be assumed that new displays are produced or exhibitions staged to showcase new research or expert study, enabling the appreciation and understanding of a new subject, angle or aspect.[22] Sometimes the findings of research into objects will provide the inspiration, yet it is equally possible for research about a person, event or period in time to be the driving force.[23] Themes for exhibitions and displays are inspired by public interest and demand, and can also therefore be market-driven. Examples might include recent political events, a hotly debated contemporary issue, the popularity of a particular artist or an historical person, or a popular cultural movement.[24]

Ideally, all the above methods of generating ideas for displays and exhibitions should be employed in combination: it is in the interests of any museum that exhibitions appeal to the interests of the public and can link to contemporary themes, communities and varied audiences.[25] Ideally, decisions about a museum's exhibition programme should be closely linked to the priorities for the museum's research activity as set out in a research policy (see Chapter 9). A museum will then be able to develop a long-term exhibition strategy over many years, with ideas generated by committee based on this research plan.

Concept and content development

Researching, developing and agreeing the nature and form of a display or exhibition, the content and type of interpretation and the objects to be included can be a significant undertaking.[26] Often, a curator is responsible for initial concept and content development, but they may be supported by expertise from historians, researchers, interpretive planners, visitor experience specialists, educators and archivists.[27]

Before and during the creation of a display or exhibition the following aspects should be considered, defined and planned:

- Purpose or focus and scope: Why this project? What is the display all about? What are the educational goals?
- Potential and intended audiences.
- Concept; the messages and storylines: What is the story we are trying to tell? What themes will be used?
- Voice, lens and tone: How will the messages be delivered, through what lens, and using what voice and tone?
- Which objects will inform and shape, as well as deliver, the concept? How will they help to tell the stories?
- Setting: What will the display or exhibition look and feel like?
- Evaluation: How and when will evaluation happen, will this be front-end, formative and/or summative evaluation?

Good quality and successful displays are unlikely to be ones where objects have simply been selected to fit a desired theme and arranged in the museum's spaces. Instead, they arise from a commitment to in-depth historical or scientific research using both primary and secondary sources of information, and the resulting identification of themes, subthemes, threads, connections and storylines.[28] Careful and expert research is therefore an essential requirement in the production of museum exhibitions and displays, and must happen throughout the development, planning and design stages of the project.[29]

Object selection is usually undertaken once the concept for the display has been confirmed and some research carried out. Frequently, this part of the process is undertaken by the curatorial team, who consider the different sections of the display and have in-depth knowledge of the collections.[30] It may be that the selected objects assist visitors in understanding the themes and ideas of the display, or alternatively that the themes and ideas showcase the objects on display.

Types of museum display

In the 'Museum Age' from the 1840s to the 1890s (see Chapter 1), collections grew rapidly, and it was common practice to display large numbers of objects in museum spaces in attempts to show as many examples and specimens as possible. Today, museums take a more focussed and discriminating approach to displays, one led by narrative and theme. Using a few carefully selected and interpreted objects can convey information and ideas much more effectively (and create a more memorable visitor experience) than a display crammed full of objects and accompanying devices. The percentage of objects on display tends to vary by museum type, but overall most museums will only show 5–15 per cent of their entire collections in specially curated galleries.[31]

It is, however, possible to display too few objects and to provide too little information about them. Some museums can focus so much on ambience, design and artistry that the objects themselves and the educational origins of the organisation are somewhat lost. A careful balance must be struck between enabling access to a reasonable number of objects and creating meaningful visitor experiences.

The approach to the display of objects in museums has been described and categorised by many different people in a variety of different ways according to the display's purpose, audience, subject, objects, interpretation, design or arrangement. Any of the methods of display outlined below might be employed by any kind of museum, and most exhibitions and displays use a mixture of styles for a variety of purposes.[32] Each museum must decide on the most appropriate method for its spaces.[33]

AESTHETIC OR CONTEMPLATIVE

This approach is most often found in art museums but can also be adopted by other types of museums. With such an approach, works of art, images, objects or specimens can be displayed and appreciated for their beauty and interest, meaning and qualities, without any contextual material.[34] These displays tend to be low density, with objects arranged in a linear sequence in order of date or of stylistic development. It is common to offer limited detail in the accompanying interpretation. Audio tours and hand-held digital devices with didactic or interactive elements can enhance the amount of information on offer, as can person-led tours.

CONCEPTUAL, CONTEXTUAL, THEMATIC OR DIDACTIC

These approaches are more likely to be found in history and science museums, where objects are intended to be seen in context and collectively tell a story, communicate an idea or subject, or enable exploration of an overall narrative or theme.[35] These displays might be arranged in a linear manner, and follow a storyline or series of relationships over time. Objects might be more numerous and more densely displayed than in contemplative approaches. Interpretation is likely be layered and several different methods might be employed. The visitor is given opportunities to examine and compare objects, explore relationships between them, and discover meanings.

A method of presentation referred to as 'process' is connected to this approach: employing storytelling and contextual information to communicate how something works, the process of making, or to explore why something happens.[36] The process approach is often seen in science museums.

SYSTEMATIC

Systematic displays tend to be found in science and natural history museums, where comprehensive collections of specimens have been built up over time and arranged in a systematic way. The displays might address a particular subject, topic or type, or might examine change over time and relationships between various specimens. This approach can sometimes be the least interesting to general visitors, but it is beneficial to experts and for use in specialist teaching.[37]

More recently, many museums have enabled public access to stored collections.[38] These 'open' or 'accessible' stores can be invaluable adjuncts to the more 'curated' display areas, allowing greater public access to objects arranged in a systematic manner, perhaps grouped together according to type, material or size.

DISCOVERY

Objects in an open store, or in the primary display areas of the museum, may be displayed without any sequence or order, allowing observations and connections that do not require consecutive links to be made. Open stores are often most successful when they can be transformed into 'discovery centres': places in which the visitor is encouraged to explore the specimens or objects and to discover meanings for themselves.[39] Interpretation may be provided in limited detail and more information might be available in the form of links to a digital catalogue or perhaps a person-led tour.

ENVIRONMENTAL, HABITAT, ASSOCIATION OR RECONSTRUCTION

This approach tends to feature dense displays of different kinds of objects arranged in a believable way and/or an imaginary environment to recreate a moment in time or particular habitat. They might be shown in a display case, or in settings through which visitors can walk. The experience might even be an entire building or site. Such displays are most usual in natural history museums and social history museums. Linked to this approach is the 'room setting', used in social history museums, historic properties or in situations when recreations of interiors are called for.

INTERACTION AND PARTICIPATION

Some displays encourage visitors to engage in kinaesthetic interaction and dialogue: that might be with interpretive apparatus (physical or digital); objects designated for handling or replicas; or staff or volunteers as guides, interpreters and demonstrators. This kind of approach is employed most often in science museums but can be equally as powerful in history museums. Visitors can also be involved in creating and curating content in a 'participatory' approach (this idea is explored further in Chapter 8).[40]

Design of displays

As well as considering narration and theme, it is also important for museums to arrange the display spaces, objects, facts, ideas and messages in an appealing, logical and accessible way, so that the audience can access them physically and interact effectively with them.[41] Doing so will enhance the ability of the museum to provide an entertaining and stimulating experience; communicate messages about objects and subjects to a range of visitors so they can explore subjects presented by the museum at their own pace and at a depth that matches their interests, expertise or identity.[42]

Messages are conveyed in museums through design and visual communication: balancing the arrangement and representation of objects, layout and visual principles in a display is essential to ensure the defined goals of a project are met.[43] Visitors might engage with objects in museums, and have their attention held by them, in three ways:

- On a visceral level: responding to the initial impact of the object and its appearance or look and feel. This is often a rapid and surface-level judgement.
- On a behavioural level: how the object can communicate its function, performance or usability.
- On a reflective level: the thoughts, feelings or image that the object leaves the user or viewer with.[44]

If an object does not make an impact on the viewer in any of these areas then it will not be appealing and interesting to them. The way visitors interact with objects at all levels can be enhanced by the way they are displayed in the museum. Curators are not trained designers, but an understanding of some of the key elements of design is extremely useful to have when working on displays and exhibitions.[45] Certain aspects of this work are outlined below.

SPACE/INTERIOR DESIGN

A design team should consider how the museum's spaces could be used to best effect to enhance the aims of the display and visitors' understanding as well as their enjoyment. Developing the spatial elements of a display can create cohesion, convey certain meanings, moods and feelings and affect visitor responses.[46]

General considerations for space in the design of museum displays and exhibitions include:

- Where and how the display or exhibition will be introduced and narrated.
- How visitors will move around the space and/or how their movements will be controlled in a particular way.
- What orientation devices will be used to direct visitors.
- How groups of visitors might use the spaces.
- If visitors can view the objects and accompanying aspects easily and effectively.
- How bottlenecks or dead spaces might be avoided.
- What interpretation devices will be used and where.

The traditional approach to museum displays was to arrange objects, showcases and interpretation on the outside walls of rectangular rooms, perhaps also with some cases and objects in the centre. Today it is just as usual to see rooms broken up and visitors encouraged to move through a series of spaces (created through the use of screen walls, panels or divisions) and for objects to be shown in a variety of different showcases, structures and platforms at different levels.[47] Adapting and adjusting different spaces in this way can add variety and stimulation; enable a change of pace; introduce surprise and anticipation; encourage close scrutiny or curiosity; and allow different areas of the display or exhibition to be presented in different ways, perhaps creating or inspiring certain moods and emotions.[48]

We know that there are certain shared behavioural tendencies for visitors to museums in the UK and US, encouraged by cultural and societal conventions. These include, for example:

- Turning to the right upon entering a museum gallery.
- Following the right wall and devoting more attention to displays on the right side of a room.
- Stopping, and paying more attention to the first display on the right side of a gallery.
- Paying more attention to the first few objects or displays in an exhibition.
- Avoiding dark areas and sections.

- Giving less attention to objects and displays at the end of an exhibition.
- Spending more time looking at objects and displays along the shortest route to the exit.
- Being attracted to brightly coloured areas and objects, and brightly lit areas or objects.
- Finding larger objects more stimulating and noticeable.
- Experiencing museum fatigue due to mental and physical stimulation, and only being able to sustain a high level of attention for around 30 minutes.[49]

Designers can employ a variety of techniques to affect the way a visitor approaches a display or exhibition and moves around the space. They might use elements such as colour; lighting; changes in (and manipulation of) spatial arrangements; different types of lines; landmark and gateway objects; panels/captions/headline text; display cases; windows and doors; and other physical barriers to create these different approaches:[50]

- Unstructured: allowing visitors to move at their own pace and to decide their own priorities and interests. This non-directional and object-focussed approach will not lend itself easily to the creation of storylines.
- Suggested: encouraging linear or radial movements and drawing people along a certain route.[51] This gives visitors a framework but also a sense of freedom of choice. It relies heavily on the effectiveness of the design elements employed.
- Directed: more restrictive and rigid, visitors are led through the display spaces and the experience is carefully structured around the development of a subject and storylines. Visitors are given little choice of what to look at and little opportunity to exit before the end: this can sometimes result in feelings of entrapment and can create bottlenecks.[52]

The patterns of movement that visitors pursue in museum spaces can have a significant impact on their experiences. It is possible to identify trends and repeating patterns in visitor movements through visitor-flow research and visualisation, drawing on space syntax methodologies.[53] Analysis of this data can improve usage of the spaces and enable modifications that improve the visitors' overall experience.[54]

It is also important to consider space when thinking about the arrangement of objects, to increase their impact, emphasise their importance and encourage visitors to examine them.[55] Surrounding an object with too little or too much space can alter the way it is received by the viewer (for example, make it seem insignificant or cause it to be lost). How objects are arranged in relation to one another and in the space (for example, open display, cases, walls) also needs to be considered and carefully organised on all planes to enable easy viewing or access as well as visual impact.[56]

PLACEMENT AND PROTECTION OF OBJECTS

Museum displays and exhibitions contain a wide variety of objects, many of which will have specific requirements. A full assessment of the conservation and security needs of each object that will be displayed should be undertaken before design decisions are made. A full range of options should be considered to protect objects, from barriers and cases to the creation of spatial separation between the displays and visitors.[57]

Museum display cases (or showcases) have been used by museums to display objects for hundreds of years. Cases provide settings in which objects can be viewed; bridge the gap between small objects, the room and the visitor; and are useful in establishing a pattern of movement for any display space.[58] Cases also provide some degree of security for objects from theft and vandalism, and can offer a level of protection from damaging environmental factors (extreme temperatures, humidity, pests).[59] A variety of different types and specifications of display cases are available and research should be conducted to select the most appropriate type according to the intended use and budget. Ideally, museum display cases should provide sufficient physical protection to objects (i.e. be robust and stable); be lockable to ensure the security of objects; and be resistant to dust and prohibit the entry of pests. If funds are available, then cases could be provided that enable the creation of microclimates and have anti-theft alarm systems fitted.[60]

SEQUENCE, TIME AND MOTION

The passage of visitors through a display can be carefully orchestrated for maximum effect. The whole experience should draw visitors in, capture their attention and provide variety, but also hang together to provide continuity.

Consideration of how to create continuing and changing vistas, sight lines, sequences of experiences and unexpected encounters is important in all this. The use of gateway and landmark objects can assist visitors in finding a way into the display or its component sections and encourage them to engage with the wider themes and narratives. Using this technique, dramatic, important or iconic objects might be placed at key moments of the display to spark interest, or so that drama and anticipation might be built as the visitor moves towards them.[61]

LINE AND FORM

Line is the most dynamic of all elements of design: it can lead the eye, imply motion and direction, alter the proportions of a space or an object and encourage different feelings in the viewer.[62] Lines may be actual or simply sensed or implied, causing the visitors; eyes to move from one point in space to another: they can be an effective way of unifying a display and tying a composition together.

We respond to form in relation to space: in museum displays, the shape, size and volume of objects should be considered so that appropriate spaces can be created in which to show them, and they might be placed in the best position within the display (for example, placing objects at the front of, or alone in, cases will capture attention and promote interest).[63] The visual impact, weight distribution, shape or mass, and visual direction of objects and the balance between them should be carefully considered.

VALUE AND TONE

The value or tone of an object is a measure of how light or dark it is, and this can also be affected by the amount of light falling upon it. Value can add visual characteristics to an object: darker values create heaviness, whereas lighter values make objects appear lighter in weight. Enabling contrasts in value through lighting in museum displays and exhibitions can be a highly effective design tool: it can assist in establishing thematic emphasis, visual and compositional order, change visitor perceptions about the size and distance of objects, inspire different moods and feelings, attract and repel, create drama and focus attention, as well as encourage certain directional movements.[64]

COLOUR

Colours in museum spaces and displays can invoke memorable first, and often lasting, impressions and can be used to enhance the visitors' responses and experiences. Colours, and their value, can often establish and maintain continuity and pull together different elements of an exhibition.[65] Conversely, colour can be used to create variety and contrasts and increase or decrease the perceived size of spaces or change their proportions. Colour will also stimulate emotional responses and can affect the mood, reactions and thoughts of visitors. Colour intensity is a further consideration: low intensity colours usually detract less from objects than more saturated colours, thus bright colours should be used sparingly and usually only for emphasis.

TEXTURE

We do not always allow visitors to touch objects in museums, however, the texture of an object or the setting or environment in which it is shown can be sensed visually. The relationship of the textural properties of different objects and of two-dimensional effects should be carefully balanced in any display.

The design process

The level of formality involved in the process of designing a display or exhibition will vary according to the nature and size of the project; the particular culture of the organisation; the amount of staff involved; and whether it is being designed and produced in house or by an external company.

If an external design company/contractor is employed, a tendering process may be conducted. For this process an initial design brief (or interpretive plan) is supplied to interested companies and the resulting proposals are examined by the museum's project team.[66] It should include full details of the:

- Aims of the project (these might be broad or very specific).
- Nature of the project (content, timeframe, possible objects, themes, initial ideas for presentation, particular arrangements or requirements for the objects).
- Target audience and intended visitor experience.
- Space in which the display or exhibition will be housed, its dimensions and any major features or restrictions.
- Timetable and delivery date.
- Budget. This might be set by the museum in advance, or the museum might take advice from the designer as to the likely costs of the project.[67]

Once a company is appointed and contracts signed it is common to follow three main stages in the design process.[68]

1 INITIAL DESIGN/CONCEPT DESIGN

The designer(s) are shown the display space, advised on budget available, and given a brief as to the scope and nature of the project, the concept, themes, messages, intended audiences and goals for interpretation. The designer should be given a draft object list and draft content for interpretation.The design team will create draft visuals, concept sketches and diagrams indicating flow and circulation, use of space, layout and the position of all interpretation. The look and feel of the display should also be indicated at this stage (for example, suggested colours, fonts, styles, graphics, finishes and materials).[69]

2 DESIGN DEVELOPMENT

The design team will produce storyboards and deliver firm ideas for interpretation methods and layout. Floor plans, section and elevation drawings, drawings/plans for component design (for example, cases, models, dioramas, working interactives). A graphics schedule, plans for materials and finishes, lighting and signage should all be set out. Technical elements such as the integration or modification of mechanical and electrical systems, the design of any hardware and software required, and performance specifications should all be presented.[70] At this stage, estimates of costs and work plans should be finalised and agreed. During this stage final object lists and content for interpretation should be developed. Evaluation of the ideas and designs might also be carried out with potential audiences.

3 FINAL DESIGNS

Object lists and final draft content for all interpretation methods should be ready and supplied. A final design package can now be produced, illustrating every element of the display or exhibition (including how it will be constructed), a floor plan showing visitor flow, elevations, sections and subsections, the location of all objects, the design of all graphics and interpretation, lighting and audio-visual (AV) elements. Final schedules for production and costs will be set out and a timetable for production and delivery should be finalised and agreed by all parties. Once the final designs have been agreed, construction drawings and specifications can be produced, showing how the display will be built and fit within the designated space. A series of packages might be produced (for example, general building work, woodwork and fabrication, AV hardware, AV software, graphics, mount-making etc.) to be sent to potential manufacturers and suppliers.

Production of displays and exhibitions

Depending on the policy of the museum, tendering may be necessary for all, or some, aspects of the work (for example, materials and suppliers involved in the build and production of the display and its components, text, graphics, AV, lighting, installation).[71] In each case contracts must be composed to reflect the drawings, agreements and construction documents produced. Any changes made during production must be carefully monitored and negotiated by the museum's project team and the quality and cost implications considered.[72]

The construction and installation of a display or exhibition should be carefully managed according to a project schedule.[73] Meticulous preparation and planning is required to ensure the project is delivered to high standards and on time, without a risk to the museum's objects and its reputation.

7

Interpreting objects

Displaying and exhibiting objects in museums presents opportunities to tell stories about them, and to communicate ideas and information, shaping the meanings visitors attach to them.[1] Museum interpretation describes all the messages that the museum sends to audiences, be those unconscious or intended. These messages are communicated to the public in many different ways, from text and person-led tours, to digital interactives and structured activities. Today, museum interpretation focusses less on instruction and the expert voice and more on audience-centred methods that create dialogues with visitors and encourage conversations.[2] In addition, thoughtful displays can create experiences that are transformative: through the objects on display and the interpretation provided the visitor might benefit from a greater or different degree of understanding; appreciate a new level of meaning; and find their attitudes, values, opinions and perceptions about an historical or contemporary issue have altered.[3] Active discovery, free-choice learning, interactivity and participation are also ideas associated with displays and exhibitions in museums today that make for effective experiences, and that modern visitors expect.

Considering objects

Before examining the various techniques through which to communicate messages, it is worth considering what it is a curator might wish to convey about objects in a museum's collection. Curators will select an object for display because they feel it is interesting in some way; information relating to it may be of value to the visitor; or it can assist in telling a certain story. In a display, an object might simply be identified, further to this contextual information about it might be presented, and it might even be interpreted.[4] How an object is considered and interpreted within a museum will depend on factors such as the:

- Amount and type of research conducted (and when).
- Level of expertise of researchers.
- Available evidence.
- Goals and mission statement of the organisation.
- Purpose of a display (this is likely to be a cyclical relationship).

Objects bear signs and meanings, in much the same way as texts.[5] These meanings are invariably embedded in social and cultural systems, beliefs and behaviours: the meaning of material culture (objects) is constructed through shared systems of significance in societies determined by the culture and historical conditions in which it was created or used.[6] Curators try to establish these meanings and ascertain the significance of the objects in the present day, allowing visitors to consider them in different ways. In museums, objects are taken away from their place of origin, detached from their original social function, given special privileged status, removed from the normal world in which objects circulate, and new given values in regard to their care, use, ownership and storage. Thus, visitors' experiences are invariably affected by the meanings and values the objects have been given by the museum.

Furthermore, museums provide access to physical objects and enable visitors to explore their worlds through considering the relationships of the objects to people, places and time. Encounters with objects can enable visitors to consider different types of human experience; gain a personal appreciation of the lives of other people, past and present; and reflect on the key aspects of being human. The concept of recording information about an object in order to compose an 'object biography' was examined in Chapter 4 and this can be useful in thinking about the agency of objects and the way social interactions between people and objects create meaning (as well as how these meanings can shift and change over time).[7] Considering the life stories of objects and their relation to one another and to humans is a useful way to position and explore them within a display or other project within the museum.

For every object in a museum's collection, further research will need to be undertaken to examine and record:

- The biography of the creator/author/artist.
- The biography of the object before and after inclusion in the collection (for example, who owned it, how, when and where).
- The story of the individual material elements.
- The production, design and distribution of the object.
- The use, exchange, alteration, movement and destruction or preservation of the object.
- The organisations, institutions and individuals associated with the object.
- The contemporary connections of people and place to the object.[8]

Considering an object using different approaches can help in assigning alternative values, meanings and richer or more original narratives and enable visitors to examine a wider range of subjects and ideas. It is tempting to consider an object primarily in terms of its function and its age, and to produce interpretation based on this aspect of its nature, but objects should also be considered using alternative approaches, for example:

- Idea or invention: the technology and concepts involved in the design and manufacture of the object.
- Design: the materials and decoration used to produce the object, its cost, association, style and function.
- Materials: the materials that were used to make the object, where are they from, why were they used?
- Marketing: the economic history of the object.
- Manufacture or production: for whom, by whom, why, where, how, when was this object made?
- Use: why and when was this object used, what for and by whom, what was its function or purpose, how has this changed over time?

- Art: the aesthetic significance of the object, its stylistic features.
- Association: what public, personal, and social connections does this object have, how has this changed over time and with different cultures, does the object have symbolic significance?[9]

This list is not intended to be exhaustive, and there will be many other theoretical perspectives and methodologies through which objects can be considered and examined, depending on the aims of any research or programme in which the object will be used (for example, taking an approach situated within the fields of public, local, economic, social, gender, family, colonial or military history, or the history of religion, education, science and medicine).

Objects can be starting points for research, reference and entertainment, inspiring museum visitors to consider and question new information and perspectives.[10] Ken Arnold considers how early museums were formed to gather together objects to study and to make enquiries about the world, to wonder, investigate and experiment. Arnold asserts that museums ought to return to these principles in the way they present objects, to create dialogue, connections, facilitate curious surprise and reignite wonder in objects and stories. We should consider using objects to tell stories and to enable knowledge creation in dialogue with the visitor through approaches that are exploratory, imaginative and experimental.[11]

Interpretation planning

When used in museums, the term interpretation is wide-ranging and all-encompassing, generally describing the way objects have been explained, the themes and subjects presented, and all the methods or tools the museum has devised and implemented to communicate the information and ideas.[12] Effective communication will only occur if museum staff have undertaken careful planning to ascertain:

- The stories and messages they want to tell, the meanings they wish to communicate and what it is they hope visitors will learn from the displays or what impact they hope the messages will have (communication objectives).[13]
- Who they wish to communicate these meanings to (audience(s)).

- How the objects in the collections can tell these stories.
- What the most appropriate ways of communicating these stores and messages are (which media they will use).[14]

In order to address these issues, ensure the objects and subjects will be received by visitors in the best way possible, and to create high-quality visitor experiences, a museum should devise an interpretive plan. This core policy will assist the museum in finding the most effective and appropriate ways to communicate with their specific audiences; ensure it takes a visitor-centred approach to create experiences that serve the interests and needs of its communities; and bring structure and formality to the nature, content and production of any project it undertakes.[15]

Some larger organisations may have one overarching interpretive strategy or plan that will set out the museum's wholesale approach to interpretation, style, graphics, text and other methods of communication, closely tied to the organisation's overall goals and mission.[16] There may even be a dedicated member of staff or department with responsibility for implementing a unified approach to interpretation methods and design across the entire museum.[17] Individual interpretive plans might be devised for individual projects and are often essential to the planning, execution, monitoring and evaluation of displays, exhibitions and learning programmes.[18]

Who produces the content for interpretation depends on the nature of the museum, its staff, and the displays or exhibitions it stages. In large museums, or for large projects, a subject-specialist or curator may carry out the research, which is then handed over to an interpretive planner or expert writer who will compose the content for any interpretation.[19]

Strategies for interpretation

In 1957, Freeman Tilden published his now famous 'six principles of interpretation'. These principles remain relevant today, and are useful to consider when developing interpretation in a range of venues and projects:

1 Any interpretation that does not somehow relate what is being displayed or described to something within the personality or experience of the visitor will be sterile.

2 Information, as such, is not Interpretation. Interpretation is revelation based upon information. But they are entirely different things. However, all interpretation includes information.
3 Interpretation is an art, which combines many arts, whether the materials presented are scientific, historical or architectural. Any art is in some degree teachable.
4 The chief aim of Interpretation is not instruction, but provocation.
5 Interpretation should aim to present a whole rather than a part, and must address itself to the whole man rather than any phase.
6 Interpretation addressed to children (say up to the age of twelve) should not be a dilution of the presentation to adults, but should follow a fundamentally different approach. To be at its best it will require a separate program.[20]

Most museum visitors expect an informal learning experience as well as a certain element of enjoyment when they visit a museum.[21] The interpretation that a museum produces, in whatever form, should be easily comprehended and digested, informal, and accessible to all: what we present to visitors in museum galleries therefore cannot be an academic thesis. A sufficient quantity and quality of information should be provided, but instead of attempting to force visitors to think in a certain way, or preach and lecture, museums should create environments that encourage close observation, exploration and discovery and enable visitors to make their own judgements, potentially transforming their awareness, perceptions, attitudes and values.[22] Enjoyment is a common expectation of museum visitors and today most museums employ interpretive techniques that create enjoyable experiences in addition to facilitating and enhancing learning.

It is equally important to remember that most museums were founded as places of education and learning and so any interpretive strategies should also aim to be in keeping with this core mission. Even visitors who are primarily seeking recreation and entertainment will want to be able to access some kind of information about the displays and objects.[23] However, visitors will not have unlimited time to spend reading long and difficult discussion pieces. Instead, the interpretation provided needs to be simple and effective, supporting, rather than distracting from, the objects on display.[24] Finding effective ways to layer information, to ease visitors into the content and to allow them to read more or less of it as they wish, is key.

We cannot control exactly how visitors respond to interpretation in museums: they will not read everything, but will dip in and out of the information given and frequently ignore the order it is presented in. Research by George Hein and Beverley Serrell highlights some key problems museums encounter, namely that visitors:

- Usually stop at less than half of the components in an exhibition.
- Spend limited time at individual exhibition components.
- Skip many elements entirely.
- Read labels less often than staff might hope.
- Spend much less time with displays and exhibitions than we think.
- Struggle to maintain attention spans which reduce after about half an hour.[25]

In order to overcome some of these challenges, a thematic framework should be developed for displays or exhibitions, outlining the themes and subthemes into which information will be grouped and presented.[26] A museum need not have one single theme or topic for its entire interpretation. Yet for individual galleries, or groups of galleries, visitors will have a richer experience and gain more educational benefit if the interpretation is linked to one overarching idea and narrative.[27]

A museum might decide to create an exhibition as a linear or nonlinear experience. A linear structure will mean the display has a beginning and end, and visitors will be encouraged to view certain elements in a controlled and fixed order. The intention is that each section of information will build on the last, until all sections come together to create a final product. It might be that the linear experience is created through a chronology or spatial relationships (for example, moving through a building or experiencing a journey).[28] A non-linear arrangement (sometimes called thematic or contextual) allows visitors to encounter and explore content in no particular order. Suggested pathways might be integrated into the design of the display, but visitors are able to move non-sequentially. Nonlinear experiences might be:

- Focal specific: one central theme or subject from which other subthemes radiate.
- Parallel thematic: certain themes or subthemes used repeatedly in different sections of the display.

- Independent structures: one gallery or area might display subjects that are unconnected or only broadly related, each section able to be viewed independently.[29]

Methods of interpretation

Interpretation produced by a museum, regardless of the medium, should link to its overall mission, aims and strategy. Curators need to consider carefully what kinds of interpretive methods might be most effective for particular collections, objects, displays and subjects and if different kinds of interpretation might be more effective for different kinds of visitors. The purpose of each method should be fully established before it is composed and the audience(s) it will serve clearly defined and catered for. The design of interpretation may also be influenced by the museum's aims in wider visitor engagement, audience development, visibility, and even income generation. Balancing the education and public engagement function of the museum with the need to raise money is not always easy.

In the past, museums tended to rely heavily on text as the primary means to provide information about the objects on display. Research has shown that visitors are more likely to engage with information and be able to retain messages when a wider range of interpretive methods are used, rather than text alone.[30] Visitors will vary in their interests and learning styles, and it is wise for museums to devise different interpretive methods that can appeal to these different approaches and link to their personal experiences (see Chapter 8, Museum audiences and learning).[31] Even if labels and text panels are chosen as the predominant method, the content can be delivered through different presentation styles (for example, conceptual, graphic, interactive, emotional, physical).[32] It is also in the interests of museums to be inspired by developments in other sectors and incorporate them into museum interpretation (for example, costumed interpretation, multimedia elements, digital content).[33]

Some interpretation is direct, some more indirect, and some techniques are more complicated or elaborate than others. Importantly, the interpretive tools provided should not detract from the objects themselves, but rather encourage curiosity for them.[34] Sometimes techniques are divided into categories of 'static' and 'dynamic'.[35] Static methods of interpretation are those which provide visitors with information, generally through one-way (rather than two-way) forms of communication:

- Text/captions/labels.
- Models.
- Maps.
- Drawings.
- Photographs (can also be museum objects).
- Booklets.
- Flyers/leaflets/information sheets.
- Catalogues.
- Dioramas/tableaux.
- Themed trails or quizzes.
- Worksheets.

Dynamic methods of interpretation often involve visitor participation and encourage the use of multiple senses with hands-on experience and the use of multimedia. They can broaden and enhance the visitors' experiences and increase opportunities to learn:[36]

- Audio.
- Video and animations.
- Guided tours.
- Lectures.
- Handling objects.
- Working models/animatronics.
- Activity sessions.
- Demonstrations.
- Education events.
- First person tours.
- Costumed/live interpretation.
- Recreations.
- Living history.
- Websites.
- Social media.
- Public collections catalogues.
- Digital interactives.
- Digital games.
- Augmented reality.
- Virtual reality.

- Data visualisation.
- Immersive spaces.
- Site-specific performances.

Other considerations include the:

- Purpose of the interpretation (see above, Interpretation planning).
- Needs of audiences (see above, Interpretation planning).
- Cost: some methods will be cheaper than others, some simply too expensive for smaller museums.
- Impact on the physical condition of museum objects. For example, if they will increase light exposure, or the materials from which they are made will cause damage to the object.
- Use and accessibility: if the techniques chosen are ones visitors will be familiar and feel comfortable with.
- Participation: visitors tend to learn more readily if they can be involved and participate in active learning, rather than just being receivers of messages.
- Sustainability: the future of the technique should be considered and thought given as to how often the content or technology will need to be updated, or components replenished or refreshed. Whether the technique relies on the particular expertise of a member of staff is also something to plan for.

Ideally, all outputs from all departments should be consistent and combine to create a unified image of the museum; there might even be an agreed house style (particularly the case for larger museums).

It is essential that interpretation is accessible to as wide a range of visitors as possible. A layered approach can be useful: limited content might be provided for immediate access (for example, object labels), but more information may be offered in other forms for those who wish to know more (for example, a website). Adaptive devices and alternative methods of interpretation that can cater for visitors with specific physical, sensory and cognitive needs (for example, large-print captions, tactile models, sign language interpretation, audio descriptions) should be provided where possible.

Museum text

Labels, captions and other text are some of the most traditional and commonly used forms of interpretation in a museum.[37] Effective text can:

- Help visitors to negotiate a gallery or a display.
- Establish a structure for the information being presented.
- Provide information about an object or group of objects, connecting it to the overall storyline.

Museum visitors will not have the time, energy or inclination to read vast amounts of complicated text, and do not want to feel overwhelmed by it: numerous studies have shown that visitors spend very little time reading individual captions and text panels.[38] But text can still be an invaluable part of a museum display:

- Attracting visitors, encouraging them to look at objects or content.
- Providing answers to questions that visitors might have about the subjects presented in the museum.
- Correcting misconceptions or misunderstandings.
- Encouraging visitors to pay active attention while in the museum.
- Connecting information presented to familiar experiences or knowledge.
- Enabling visitors to draw analogies and transforming ideas into stories.[39]

It is important to think about the content, design and positioning of all text included in a display.[40] Text elements need to work together to achieve the aims of the interpretive plan (for example, tell a story, showcase an object(s), explore an idea or concept), and they should always be written with particular audience(s) in mind.[41] Text should have an obvious order, structure and hierarchy (including, for example, headline text, introductory panels, theme/group/section panels, case panels and object labels).[42] Such a hierarchy, making a clear distinction between different types of text, helps visitors to find the information they want more quickly and easily. The exact nature of this hierarchy, format, layout and structure of text panels, and their word limits, will vary between organisations, and sometimes between different displays or exhibitions within the same museum. It is important not to stray from this hierarchy once it has been established for a particular display, though of course a redisplay may provide the opportunity to revise the museum's policies.[43]

Presentation of museum text

The presentation of text, and the way it is organised, should be consistent in elements such as typeface, colour, size and placement. Displays that are cohesive, clear and professionally presented will assist visitors in engaging with the objects on show and understanding the messages the museum is attempting to communicate.[44] Text should be as legible as possible and accessible to many different visitors. Below is a selection of suggested guidelines:[45]

- Use a sans serif font (for example, Arial and Verdana).
- Avoid decorative fonts, except perhaps for main headings if it seems appropriate for the subject of the display.
- Use the same typeface throughout.
- Choose an appropriate size text that can be read by as wide a range of visitors as possible at a distance (the choice of size will depend on where the text will be placed).
- Use different sized text for different types of label.
- Left align text.
- Leave room for a margin around the text on any label or text panel.
- Limit lines of text to around 50–60 characters.
- Do not hyphenate words at the end of lines.
- Do not use upper case, bold or italic text, except perhaps for a brief title or for special emphasis.
- Avoid using pastel shades or coloured inks: in general, the most accessible and effective colour for museum text is a white, or off-white, background with black (or similarly dark) text.
- Do not wrap text around objects or walls.
- Do not superimpose text on a busy background image.
- Avoid materials that will result in glare or reflection.
- Avoid placing text where it will be in shadow, in a tight corner, or obscuring the view of an object (either directly, or by visitors reading another text).

- Position text panels and labels at a height so that they can be seen by as many different visitors as possible.
- Provide sufficient light to read the text.
- Be consistent in placement of panels and labels within the display, and make sure they are positioned near the object they relate to. Careful consideration should be given to possible banking of several labels together, below or to one side of objects, perhaps with corresponding reference numbers. This can avoid overwhelming small objects but can also mean undue effort is required from visitors to match the object with its label.
- Ensure labels are legible for people with visual impairments, or ensure alternative formats are available.[46]

Content of museum text

Writing museum text that works for visitors needs careful consideration and can be a difficult task for a curator who has extensive expert knowledge. The audience(s) that the display is aimed at should always be considered when composing text: their level of knowledge, education, and particular characteristics will determine the nature and presentation of the content.[47] Writing effective text requires practice and dedication: ideally it should convey all the relevant information in a concise, clear and understandable way, provoke curiosity and motivate visitors to continue looking at the displays, without being vague or oversimplified.[48]

Many authors have produced guidelines on the most effective ways to write museum text; some of the most essential points are presented here:[49]

- Text should attract the visitor's attention and make them want to learn more about a subject.
- It is often a good idea to make reference to something about the objects on display, connecting them to the written content and encouraging visitors to look at them.
- Content should be presented in an active voice, using a simple, conversational, flowing and direct approach.
- Content should provoke and stimulate the visitors' ability to think and learn.[50]

- Information provided should be relevant and clear, allowing for ease of reading and straightforward comprehension.
- A visitor is unlikely to read all text elements in a display, or in the order intended: each text element should therefore be able to be read independently.
- All content should be organised logically, and with an obvious order (the text hierarchy will help with this, and it may be a good idea to use titles and subtitles).
- Text might be accompanied by graphics, diagrams, models or photographs to create more interest and enable the viewer to use their other senses.
- It is good practice to create text for a reading age of around 12–13 (though this may rise to 15 years for supplementary information or for content aimed at a more specialist audience).[51]
- Expert knowledge must be shaped and distilled in order to appeal, to and be understood by, a non-specialist general public. Expert-only words, technical terms, scientific names, long or unfamiliar words should be avoided.[52]
- Clauses, long phrases and compound sentences should be minimised, and lengthy or complicated text broken down into smaller sections. Similarly, alliteration, exclamation points and quotations can sometimes be effective, but should be used sparingly and only when they advance the narrative.[53]
- Obscure references; metaphors or assumptions about lifestyle; jokes and colloquial phrases, or ones that might exclude and alienate certain types of visitor, should be avoided.
- Content should reflect the interests, life experiences, culture, ethnicity and socio-economic position of a wide range of people.[54]
- Museums should ensure that content changes with the times and is in-tune with the values and concerns of society and reflects the attitudes of a wide variety of visitors.[55]
- Interactivity might be included (for example, in the form of questions, problems or challenges), encouraging dialogue between the visitor and the curator and allowing visitors to discover things for themselves.[56]
- Content might be created that conveys moods, feelings and explores attitudes and beliefs.

- Alternative approaches to the production of content might be considered: for example, working with visitors to produce the content, or allowing them to respond to it and create their own.[57]

Audio and visual methods/digital technology/multimedia

The use of audio and/or video in museums is commonplace, and the range of possible techniques that might be included in this category is wide. AV tools can add much to a display or exhibition and can have a variety of functions. A high-quality AV product can, however, sometimes be expensive to commission, install and in some cases to run and maintain. Their function in meeting the aims of the museum's interpretive strategy must therefore be carefully considered.[58]

Audio guides are the most traditional method in this category, allowing visitors to move around and access information about the objects on display or within an historic building or site. Careful consideration should be given to the nature of the content for these resources and the voices used: factors such as the gender, age or accent of a speaker can have an impact on how the content is received by different audiences. Lens, tone and level of detail are also major decisions: if the content is delivered in the first or third person, by professional actors or in-house staff, and if it will be simple enough for all visitors to understand, or alternatively aimed at specialist groups.

Digital media can enhance learning by providing opportunities to communicate information about objects or subjects in different and more dynamic ways.[59] These techniques can also facilitate the creation of layers of interpretation, provide a greater depth of information and can be of great use in an interpretive approach that aims to examine context, use and/or process.[60] Examples of outputs within this category include:

- Websites.
- Animations.
- Videos.
- Games (on a console in the museum/accessible on other devices).
- Mobile apps.
- Hand-held devices (containing a combination of text, audio, animation, games etc.).

- Interactive experiences.
- Multisensory experiences.
- Immersive experiences.
- Virtual exhibitions and tours.
- Social media.
- Location-based services.
- Augmented reality.
- 360-degree videos.
- Virtual reality.
- Data visualisation.[61]

Museums should try to incorporate digital technology into displays and interpretation where possible. This might be a simple and low-cost approach, or it might be more wholesale and resource intensive. No one approach or model will fit every museum or display, and the choice will depend on the museum in question and the aims of the particular display.

The use of digital media in museums is not without its challenges. Creating digital products requires professional technical, artistic, analytical and production skills, and external contractors may need to be employed.[62] The stakes are high when so many visitors use digital tools and media on a daily basis. The amount of digital interpretation methods in a museum should be balanced with the expectations and needs of its particular audience(s): too much of this approach may alienate users who prefer more traditional methods, or who are seeking a primarily contemplative experience, or wish to explore and discover things for themselves.

Hands-on experiences

Our perceptions of, and desires for, museum spaces are changing. Visitors are no longer surprised when they are asked to use multiple senses and enter into hands-on experiences in museums. In fact, there is an increasing expectation that such activities will be on offer. Creating a sense of place can help audiences to connect with the past and gain some sense of what it might have been like: this could involve experiences in which visitors are encouraged to listen, smell, touch and perhaps even taste. Hands-on experiences might be as simple as providing demonstrations, allowing visitors to handle objects, interact with working models, or dress up in costumes. Activities such as craft sessions can help visitors to gain knowledge about how objects were made, what they were used for, and how they work, as well as the people who made and used them. Creative responses (for example, contemporary art commissions) and interactive site-specific performances (for example, immersive theatre performances) can exploit the properties, qualities and meanings of a particular physical environment (in this case a museum or historic site/building) to provide a different sort of visitor experience.

Participation and visitor contribution

Traditionally, museum interpretation has been heavily weighted in favour of the curatorial or expert voice as the primary (and often sole) authority.[63] Displays and exhibitions were considered as the means through which to showcase scholarly activity. Today, this approach is frequently challenged, and museums provide more opportunities for visitors to contribute to content and temper this interpretive authority. It is increasingly possible for multiple voices and perspectives to be represented in museum spaces. Authorship of a display or other project might be shared with external collaborators, or audiences might be asked to contribute to content. This approach can be employed in attempts to connect and involve members of communities traditionally underrepresented, or misrepresented, in museums.

Digital methods can facilitate this approach even further, allowing wider and more diverse audiences to interact with and contribute to the content of the museum, without having to be physically present. It can also enable more flexible and varied ways through which people can interact with the museum and make connections with the objects, staff and other users.[64] For example, social media platforms allow users to comment on the objects or work of the museum; online catalogues can be created with built-in options for public comment and contribution; and the public can be given the opportunity to co-create content through the museum's website (for example, blogs and virtual exhibitions).[65]

8 Museum audiences

Museums have a clear strength: they can offer unique experiences in the form of personal encounters with real objects, arousing curiosity and enabling physical connections with the past. Today, museums are no longer places for top-down instruction, where expert curators are the exclusive and authoritative voices: instead, they prioritise the user and seek to provide meaningful and relevant experiences, enabling connections, conversations and participation.[1] As Stephen Weil asserts, museums today are designed so that they are for somebody, rather than only about something.[2] This chapter explores museum audiences and learning and participation in the museum.

Museum curators have always been, and remain, educators. They are called upon to explain and present information and ideas to a range of audiences in a variety of formats, often using a variety of methods. A knowledge of how museum visitors learn, and ways through which to analyse audiences or measure the effectiveness of the museum's outputs, can greatly assist curators in this work.

The museum experience

Many different things shape a visit to a museum, affecting how visitors interact with the objects on display as well as the information the museum staff want to communicate. The museum cannot control all these factors, but it can influence some of them. Eilean Hooper-Greenhill's holistic model of museum communication highlights how elements such as the museum building, staff, orientation, shop/cafe/toilet, events and publications can all contribute to the perceptions and attitudes of visitors, and shape what kind of experience they have: it is not all about the displays and objects.[3] John Falk and Lynn Dierking assert that our experiences in a museum are effected by a combination of several different elements all working at once: the personal, social and physical context of our visit.[4] George Hein further notes that in order for museums to provide the best experience for visitors, their practical needs should first be satisfied.[5] Leisure activities are generally selected because they offer positive and affirmative experiences, ones that feel worthwhile. Museums therefore need to provide environments in which visitors feel welcome and comfortable, and enjoyable, interesting and rewarding encounters with objects, ideas and people.[6]

There is an ever-present debate in the museums sector concerning the nature of the museum as a place of entertainment as well as education. As Chapter 1 showed, many museums were originally founded as places for education, inspired by collections of objects gathered together and purposefully arranged. For most museums this wish to provide formal and informal learning experiences remains a primary undertaking. Yet museums can, and should, also be places where visitors have enjoyable creative and imaginative experiences. Museums are part of the wider leisure and tourism industry and are competing with other providers for the public's leisure time: it is recognised that many visitors come to museums because they know they will have an enjoyable time.[7] Furthermore, the continued success of the museums sector and the deliberate efforts of museums to reach out to new audiences have encouraged different groups of people to visit.[8] These new visitors are unlikely to have any specialist knowledge, and are likely to be seeking content that is stimulating, enjoyable and not overly complicated. Museums should adopt and adapt many of the techniques employed in other organisations in the entertainment sector, perhaps placing more of an emphasis on experiences that are universally accessible, pleasurable and even spectacular. Museums today are also generally more likely to explore commercial possibilities connected to their activities: for example, shops, corporate sponsorship, corporate hire, and blockbuster exhibitions.

On the other hand, we know that many visitors will come to a museum seeking an encounter with real objects, and an experience that is authentic. That might be the opportunity to see a much-admired work by a named artist, an object or place associated with an historical event or personality, or it might be the ability to explore and understand a theory or idea through interactive apparatus (physical or digital) or an activity.[9] Still other visitors may be seeking a more simple and contemplative experience or an opportunity to connect with objects without wishing to access any interpretation or interactive content.

As a result of these complementary, rather than contradictory, roles of the contemporary museum, displays and exhibitions (often produced by curators) should aim to be both educational and entertaining. The particular balance between education and entertainment in the content and activities of any museum needs to be carefully considered, and should be appropriate to the type of museum; the kind of visitors the museum already has and wishes to attract in the future; its mission and the main themes it aims to explore; and the nature of the objects in the collections.[10]

The use of objects in museum education

Curators generally have responsibility for the objects held by the museum in which they work. While exhibitions and displays are a key way that museum objects can be used, they can inspire and support a wide range of other activities. It is important that curators familiarise themselves with a range of other ways to encourage access to museum objects and interaction with them.

Through the majority of their activities, museums provide the opportunity for learning. The term 'education programme' or 'education department' has often been used in the past to refer to a formal programme of sessions and events for schools, children and their parents in museums.[11] While this restricted definition is now outdated, formal and structured museum learning or education programmes can help a museum to focus its efforts and they remain key outputs for most organisations.[12] These programmes should not, however, be designed and delivered just for children and school groups: individuals of all ages, backgrounds and circumstances can benefit from learning experiences in the museum, and should be catered for.[13] Furthermore, museums are not places in which learning is delivered in the same way as in schools. Instead, they are places of informal, free-choice learning where visitors are invited to take their own direction and learn at their own pace, thus a more varied programme of delivery is possible than in more formal settings.[14] Another strength of learning activities in museums is that they can be delivered through approaches that are effective and enable audiences to explore their feelings, attitudes, beliefs and values.[15]

Museum objects can be starting points for a wide range of activities for users of all ages, and museum curators may draw on their knowledge to plan and produce some or all of the following:

- Lectures, talks and demonstrations, either in the museum or in external locations.
- Courses, workshops and activity sessions (enabling the acquisition of new skills or a creative output).
- Guided walks or field trips/discovery trips.
- Schools sessions led by museum staff.
- Self-directed school or other group visits using resources prepared by the museum.
- Object loans to schools or other local groups (for example, hospitals, elderly users, societies, communities in remote locations).
- Competitions and quizzes/learning games.
- Educational demonstrations.
- Performances (such as dance and theatre) and role playing.
- Historical recreations and re-enactments.
- Special interest group sessions.
- Training for museum professionals.[16]

There is no one model to fit every museum, and each programme must be in keeping and complementary to the nature of the museum, its overall themes, mission and direction, its collections, space, staff expertise, intended audiences and financial resources.[17]

Some museums will have sufficient resources to employ specialist learning staff to devise and deliver learning programmes. In smaller organisations this work may need to be carried out by other staff in partnership with external contractors and volunteers: it is therefore important that a curator retains at least a basic knowledge of the planning and delivery of learning sessions.[18] Some museums may be able to assign designated spaces in which 'learning sessions' can take place: care should be taken to ensure these spaces do not become disconnected from the museum's displays and collections and reserved as areas for the exclusive use of children and schools.

Museum audiences and learning

Operating in a more visitor-focussed manner and creating experiences, activities and 'products' that audiences might like to use, more than once, will be of benefit to any museum. Museum staff, including curators, should take action to understand visitors, their needs and interests: what visitors want is not always the experience museum staff deliver.[19] Such research can also help the museum consider how it markets itself and to whom and ensure its future survival by strengthening its cultural relevance.

Designing content and experiences that serve audiences can be supported and enhanced through an understanding of how people learn in museums, the ways through which audiences might receive and construct knowledge, and their needs and expectations in this area.[20] Many specialists have devised theories to help us understand how people learn, and these have been influential in the development of museum experiences: these include theories of behaviourism, constructivist learning, active learning, experiential learning, enquiry-based learning and social cognition.[21] An understanding of these theories, and appreciation of how their adoption in the activity of the museum can strengthen its educational and interpretive outputs, will assist curators in their work as educators.

Cognitive development and constructivist learning theories propose we learn by actively constructing our own knowledge and are able to learn more readily if we are able to experiment and find our own answers, connecting new knowledge to old.[22] Museums are places where this kind of learning can happen.[23] Hein asserts that museums can adopt these learning theories and enable visitors to connect what they already know with the new things they see, do and encounter on their visit: the 'constructivist museum'.[24] Experiential learning theories suggest that knowledge is created through the cycle of transforming lived experience into current patterns of thinking, a direct encounter, rather than just a consideration of the idea in theory.[25] Museums are places in which this type of learning happens, and such encounters can be facilitated.[26]

Museums should also create experiences that draw on theories of discovery learning, enquiry-based and problem-based learning. All involve the learner undertaking self-directed enquiry in order to develop their thinking and learning skills, facilitating the real-world application of social and cultural knowledge. Such experiential and authentic learning contexts can be strengthened by problem-based learning techniques, where students attempt to solve problems at their own pace that are realistic and apply to real-life situations.[27] Encouraging curiosity and experimentation can also be an effective approach to learning: research suggests that 'arousing curiosity' can make learning more rewarding and pleasurable and assist in the recall of information.[28]

Environments outside of the formal classroom often provide more opportunities for learners to interact socially, and some of these interactions can promote various types of learning and skills development.[29] Proponents of this theory suggest when information is disseminated and processed cooperatively and collaboratively between learners (and the instructor) within a 'community of practice', learning is more effective.[30]

Howard Gardner's multiple intelligences theory, suggesting that humans possess many forms of intelligence, is popular with educators and has encouraged interest in other forms of intelligence beyond just that of verbal-linguistic and logical-mathematical, and delivering teaching using a wider range of methods, adapting it to individual strengths. This theory suggests that we can learn in many different ways, and that some people may learn more easily via one or more of the following methods:

1 Musical-rhythmic (music, melody, rhythm).
2 Visual-spatial (images, using space, imagination).
3 Verbal-linguistic (words, talking, writing, reading).
4 Logical-mathematical (numbers, logical thought, problem solving).
5 Bodily-kinaesthetic (physical experiences, doing, moving, touching).
6 Interpersonal (social experiences, communicating with others).
7 Intrapersonal (self-reflection, objectivity).
8 Naturalistic (creative, natural world, connection to nature).
9 Existential [2009 update] (information not available to the senses).[31]

Gardner also theorises that learners can access subjects through five different 'entry points' or distinct approaches, ones they feel able and comfortable in accessing. Museums can use this information to provide different types of activities and opportunities for visitors to engage with subjects in different ways, appealing to a variety of learning styles.[32]

1 Aesthetic: reacting to the formal and sensory qualities of an object or subject.
2 Narrative: responding to narrative elements of a subject or object.
3 Logical/quantitative: engaging with something through using deductive reasoning or numerical considerations.
4 Foundational: a consideration of the broader concepts and philosophical issues.
5 Experiential: responding to a subject or object by doing something with hands or bodies.[33]

Effective interpretation and learning activities in the museum will combine linear, structured or didactic approaches with dynamic, interactive, multimedia and multisensory techniques, and opportunities to engage in participatory and social learning.[34]

Understanding and developing museum audiences

Not all museum visitors are the same: there will be variety in age, gender, ethnicity, nationality, social group, educational level, religion, interests, values and attitudes. Museum audiences will be a collection of distinct and discrete groups, who will act and think in different ways.[35] Building a clear picture of the museum's audiences (who they are, what they know, how they act and how they learn in a place like a museum) can assist curators and other museum staff in creating experiences for visitors that are meaningful, enjoyable, and that they will want to engage with.[36] It can also help to determine the level of demand for the museum's current services, who uses them, and how they could be improved.[37]

It is also essential that museums serve as wide a range of people as possible and develop their ability to attract new audiences. We know that participation in museums is not spread equally across populations: some people are less likely to visit museums and take part than others (for example, those from lower socio-economic backgrounds or from minority groups). Many museums were founded with the aim to enable public access to educational experiences, and this access should not just be for select audiences. This means making concerted efforts to engage with those who do not already use the museum and who may have been overlooked in the past.[38] This market research should feed into the museum's forward plan and marketing plan, and a formal Audience Development Plan must be developed.[39]

Categorising visitors and audience segmentation

Museums can collect data to define and profile different user groups. Segmenting and categorising groups of visitors, their needs and viewing habits in this way can help curators and other museum staff to understand their audiences and identify their different expectations, attitudes and needs. A mixture of both quantitative and qualitative data should be gathered in order to identify trends and patterns relating to audiences based on numbers and statistics as well as behaviours and feelings.[40] This data might be collected via visitor surveys/questionnaires, interviews, comment cards/books, participatory exercises such as voting, online forums, time and motion studies, participant observation, visitor and stakeholder focus groups, and social media feedback.[41] These activities might be conducted by museum staff in house or perhaps by an external agency.

One way of examining audiences is to define certain demographic categories and divide visitors into subgroups within the categories (for example, life stage, gender, socio-economic status, place of residence, educational level, employment and cultural background). Yet demographic attributes are just one factor that may affect visitor behaviour: examining psychological criteria can help to provide a deeper understanding of users and enable attitudinal rather than behavioural segmentation. Questions directed towards users will include those designed to reveal their personality, values, attitudes, interests and lifestyles. This will help museums to understand the pre-existing experiences and knowledge that will impact on the purpose of users' visits, their concerns when they are there, and what information and ideas they will be receptive to.[42]

Another way to group museum users is to consider their motivations for visiting.[43] One of the first studies to examine what motivates visitors to come to museums in their leisure time, considering these organisations as part of the wider leisure industry, was carried out in 1983 at the Toledo Museum of Art.[44] The study highlighted certain factors that audiences prioritise when deciding on which pastimes to pursue:

- Being with people, or social interaction.
- Doing something worthwhile.
- Feeling comfortable and at ease in one's surroundings.
- Having a challenge of new experiences.
- Having an opportunity to learn.
- Participating actively.

Similarly, in 1999, Andrew Pekarik, Zahava Doering and David Karns at the Smithsonian Institute considered the type of experiences visitors might be seeking in the museum and divided them into categories according to four main motivating factors:

- Seeing real artefacts (object centred).
- Gaining information and new insights (information centred).
- Spending quality time with friends or family (social centred).
- Having a quiet, reflective, personally rewarding experience (introspective centred).[45]

Creating experiences in museums that enable visitors to find the attributes identified in both studies can help raise visitor numbers and satisfaction, encourage return visits and attract new audiences.

Other systems have been devised through which to group certain attributes, motivations, attitudes and behaviours of museum visitors and to define audience groups.[46] John Falk, for example, suggested we should think about visitors as having a range of different motivations, identities and needs that they wish to have fulfilled. Falk's model of the museum visitor experience focusses on these identity-related motivations and considers the specific reasons that visitors use to justify and organise their visit and that they bring with them:

- Explorers: these visitors are driven by curiosity, they like knowledge and are seeking more information.

- Facilitators: these users tend to be socially motivated to visit.
- Experience Seekers: these visitors see the museum as an important destination, and visits as something that 'must be done'.
- Professionals/Hobbyists: these visitors have some level of specialist knowledge.
- Rechargers: these visitors are seeking a contemplative, spiritual and/or restorative experience.[47]

Falk later added two additional categories, after observing that certain special types of museums attracted visitors with a particular identity:

- Affinity Seekers: these visitors come to a particular museum because it speaks to their sense of heritage and/or personhood.
- Respectful Pilgrims: these visitors feel a sense of duty or obligation to make a visit to the museum.[48]

Falk noted that these seven identities are not fixed, can change over time, and visitors might be more than one at a time. He suggested that his model could be used by museums to predict who might visit a museum, what they might do on their visit, and what kind of meanings and experiences they might take away from it in the long term.

There are many other ways to think about and categorise groups of museum visitors, identify why they might come (or not) to museums, and what they wish to do when they are there. Different museums will adopt different systems to consider their visitors. Some large museums or heritage organisations will have the resources to employ research agencies to undertake thorough analyses of their audiences, and to devise categories of distinct needs and requirements.[49]

Evaluating museum resources and experiences

Evaluating the activities a museum undertakes will also assist museum staff in the creation of more effective experiences. It is often the responsibility of a museum curator to ensure that evaluation is incorporated into project plans and undertaken at appropriate moments and for specific purposes, so an understanding of this activity is pertinent to their work.

Evaluation can help museums to:

- Consider what elements of their offer are working well, and what are not, as well as how these aspects worked and why.
- Take steps to repeat successes or to improve things that are not working or where mistakes have been made.
- Identify strengths and weaknesses: decide where to direct resources in future, how to improve future work and best practice.
- Show they are accountable, that the projects, programmes and activities they run are effective and fit for purpose.
- Focus efforts and provide projects with a framework and clear aims.
- Encourage a dialogue between the museum and stakeholder groups.
- Articulate the value of the work they do, not just in terms of visitor numbers or income but also the impact on visitors' lives.
- Show the value of their work to funders/sponsors/senior management and demonstrate the impact of the projects/programmes/events/activities to justify continued, or seek future, funding.

Evaluation can be undertaken for a variety of museum 'products' (for example, displays, exhibitions, learning events) and at several stages:

- Before the design and creation of a product (Front-end).
- During production (Formative).
- Once the product has been delivered and is in operation/process (Summative).[50]

Techniques through which to conduct this evaluation include focus groups with representative groups or individuals from the target audience(s), subject specialists, museum staff and other stakeholders; the use of a mock up or pilot by a sample of visitors; watching or tracking visitors; seeking direct audience feedback through interviewing at random or via focus groups; and soliciting critical appraisal from outside experts.[51] It is important to consider how and when to evaluate any project or activity at the outset, this will include a consideration of how to assess whether or not the aims have been achieved and what the measures of success will be.

Measuring impact

There is an increasing need to measure the success of the products museums deliver.[51] Measuring impact can help a museum to show its value, gain legitimacy and retain support; ensure funds and energies are being spent on the most high-quality products and services that serve the needs of users; and emphasise the museum's public and financial accountability.

Some measurements of success might rely on straightforward criteria that can be measured quantitatively:

- Visitor numbers.
- Website interactions.
- Profit gained through ticket sales and commercial activities.
- The number of objects cared for.
- The number of exhibitions delivered.
- The value of income from tourism and investment and level of regeneration of local areas the museum helps to encourage.

A museum must also be able to show how the activities it undertakes will positively impact audiences socially and intellectually. These markers of success may be more difficult to measure in short facts and figures. Museums offer unique opportunities, reflecting on the past to:

- Help visitors construct new knowledge and use it in the future.
- Widen access to, and attainment in, education (which may increase employability).
- Provide environments for free-choice learning, creative and imaginative expression and exploration.
- Encourage a passion for knowledge and learning, with opportunities to feel a sense of accomplishment.
- Offer the opportunity for visitors to interact with one another and to learn social skills.
- Assist visitors in developing new skills and abilities, self-confidence, self-awareness, self-esteem and motivation.
- Provide experiences that are transformative (for example, encouraging the exploration and adoption of new attitudes, values and ideas).

- Create opportunities for the sharing of knowledge and to inspire critical thinking, curiosity and creativity.
- Contribute to the happiness and well-being of visitors and communities.
- Encourage a sense of place, pride, belonging and of community spirit and distinctiveness.
- Help to improve the lives of isolated and marginalised people, and those with health difficulties.
- Provide opportunities for people to learn about and understand each other's lives, beliefs and differences.
- Encourage people to reflect on contemporary society, current affairs, ethical issues, issues of social justice and human rights, equality and diversity, discrimination, and to work towards a better future.
- Help to protect the natural environment and address climate change.[53]

Measuring and articulating the value of many of the potential outcomes named above can be extremely challenging, especially when they involve intangible and subjective benefits. Museums must try to be innovative and devise a range of ways to do this.

Active participation

The way museums communicate with visitors, and invite audiences to interact with them, has changed: we no longer rely on purely didactic forms of delivering learning such as lectures and demonstrations. In general, humans prefer experiences that involve active participation, rather than passive observation. The benefits of experiential learning or 'learning by doing' can be gained through pursuit of certain activities in the museum, for example, object handling and hands-on activities.[54]

Participating in museum experiences can go further than this: visitors expect the same opportunities for personalised social engagement and active participation that they might find in other organisations and activities.[55] To be successful and thrive, indeed sometimes simply to exist, museums must take steps to involve the public who often provide the funding for them in the form of taxes, donations and entrance charges. Today, the public are increasingly willing, able and eager to participate and be involved in the construction of knowledge and the exchange of ideas, rather than act as passive recipients of 'official' information from the museum as the only 'purveyor of truth' or 'cultural authority'.[56]

Museum curators should recognise and embrace this preference from the public for participation and co-production, and work to ensure the outputs they devise and deliver reflect these changes. This approach does not mean that a museum must implement a wholesale step-change, entirely abandoning existing methods of display, exhibition and interpretation. Successful museum displays are those that provide ways through which visitors can explore content for themselves; discover and select meanings without being instructed and told what to think; interact with, and relate to the topics, ideas, one another and the museum staff before, during and after the visit; participate in both an intellectual and physical or sensual way in the construction of new knowledge; feel a connection to their own interests and concerns; and use their imaginations and explore feelings and sensations.[57] The objects in the museum's collection can become starting points for conversations and reflections from community members in partnership with museum staff, so that new meanings can be constructed and dialogues created.[58]

Museum staff can invite and empower audiences to join the museum as partners and involve them more frequently and closely in the creation of content and in strategy, planning and decision-making in the museum.[59] At one end of the scale it might be that visitors are invited to leave a comment, vote, contribute their own thoughts, discuss an idea with someone else, or participate in community consultation work. On the other hand, it might be a bigger contribution: perhaps creating and delivering an art work, event or performance, co-curating an exhibition, performing some aspect of collections management, influencing an interpretation project or programme, taking action to shape and direct the course and content of an exhibition or activity, or contributing to strategic planning and decision-making. Still more ambitious schemes might enable members of the public to plan and deliver an entire exhibition or event within the museum space by themselves.[60] All this activity can strengthen the role of museums as public resources: they become democratic organisations and forums in which the interests, concerns and perspectives of the community are reflected in the activities and content of the museum.[61]

Museums today are also eager to address matters relating to inclusivity, widening participation, and empowerment. One major way that museums can enhance inclusion, work to remove barriers and open up access to the experiences they offer to wider audiences, is to ensure their objects, content and activities reflect the life experiences, traditions, interests and concerns of as broad a range of people as possible. Making museum spaces physically and intellectually accessible is also essential: minority and alternative views must be represented and spaces in which a variety of groups and people of all abilities can feel comfortable and represented should be created.

Access policies and plans

Museums are expected to make their collections and records accessible to a wide range of users, in line with their role as public institutions. Another of their core responsibilities is to preserve the objects in their care for the future. These two priorities are not always compatible with one other. The need for a museum to devise and implement a Collections Management Policy (CMP) was discussed in Chapter 4 (Collections management policies). Within the CMP will be a document outlining the museum's vision for access to collections and connecting to its users and its plans for achieving this: an Access Policy and Plan. A curator is usually responsible for devising these policies and will be tasked with finding solutions to enable a level of access, while also ensuring objects are properly cared for.

The ideas and procedures set out within an Access Policy and Access Plan will help the museum to balance its obligation to enable public access with the need to protect the collections and any data or records that may be sensitive. There are bound to be some difficult decisions to be made, and policies implemented that are intended to help protect the museum's objects, but that also curtail access in some way. The documents will outline:

- The legal framework within which the museum must operate with regard to access.
- Who can have access, to what, when, how, and for what reasons.
- Any conditions that must be applied to certain types of access (for example, level of supervision and handling, if photography is allowed).

- Any access restrictions on certain objects or information: this might include sensitive and confidential objects and records or any information that might compromise the security or status of objects and individuals.
- How access is approved, by whom, and the procedures for enabling it.
- The requirements for documenting and supervising certain types of access.
- The museum's attitude towards lending and borrowing.
- The museum's policies on copyright, intellectual property and photography of the collections.
- The limits of commercial use of the collections and the museum site.
- Any factors that might have a significant impact on the level of access possible (for example, security and conservation requirements and matters of personal safety or safeguarding vulnerable adults and children).[62]
- How the museum is ensuring the best possible physical, intellectual, social, geographical and cultural access to users of all ages, genders, ethnicities, socio-economic backgrounds, physical or mental abilities, education levels and places of residence.
- How the museum is assessing access and identifying and addressing any unnecessary barriers to access (for example, audience research, an access audit).

PART FOUR

THE MUSEUM CURATOR

9 The curator today and conclusions

Today's museums

A key movement in museology occurred in the 1970s and 1980s; academics and museum practitioners began to reflect on the function of museums and the relationship between these institutions and society.[1] This movement, known as New Museology, questioned the position and authority of museums in determining social and cultural values and meanings. It asserted that museums needed to change because they were serving the interests of only a narrow and exclusive section of society and that they were not using public money efficiently or for the good of all of society.[2] New Museology asserted that museums should move away from focussing just on the functional role of caring for collections and curatorship to take on a greater social and political role in society; become more people-focussed; serve and represent a more diverse public; and adopt new forms of communication and interactions with audiences, working in dialogue to create and exchange knowledge.[3] In 1971, Duncan Cameron argued that the museum should be both a 'temple' and a 'forum': an institution and authoritative space for official culture, but also a populist place for discussion and dialogue.[4] A few years later Kenneth Hudson suggested museums needed to question the nature of their work and move towards becoming places not just for intellectual enquiry, but also for experiences involving the emotions and the senses.[5] In 1983, Stephen Weil asserted that museums needed to find a balance between being object- or people-focussed organisations, and being research institutions or providing public education.[6]

As a result of these ideas, as well as significant political and economic pressures in the last 50 years, museums have moved away from a blinkered focus on the research and display of objects to also consider visitor experiences and interactions and to provide more visitor-oriented services.[7] While certain key founding principles and core activities such as scholarship, exploration and public education are retained, these organisations have undoubtedly evolved. Some progress has been made in rejecting the image of elite and exclusive organisations and many museums have shifted towards:

- Providing experiences that are both entertaining and educational.
- Providing greater access for wider sections of society.
- The representation of more diverse histories, cultures and ways of life in museum displays, content and activities.
- Enabling greater involvement and input from the public into museum content and services.
- The pursuit of activities that can help to tackle problems in society.[8]

While a change has occurred in what we understand as the functions of museums in modern society, the full vision of the New Museology movement has arguably not been realised in all museums and in all parts of the museums sector. Many authors have suggested that the approach has only been partially adopted, and sporadically by different nations, organisations and museum staff and assert that more must be done to achieve open and inclusive organisations that actively serve all of society.[9]

The museum workforce

The changes outlined above have inevitably affected the nature of the museum workforce, and the roles of many museum staff. As a result of their historic roles as specialist academic custodians of collections belonging to wealthy collectors or learned societies, museum curators have traditionally been considered as expert gatekeepers to collection objects, allowing access only to select visitors.[10] Thus, curators who were academics previously made up the majority of the workforce and carried out the major functions of the museum. Until the mid-20th century, scholarly research was the primary activity of many curators, with operational, administrative and public education work only secondary duties.

As museums began to identify the importance of their public role from the 1970s onwards and to question how they might better serve society, the idea of the museum profession also grew. As the number of museums rose from the mid-20th century onwards (see Chapter 1, Museums today) so did the number of people working in museums. It is difficult to estimate the total number of staff working in the museums sector worldwide or in any one country. As noted in Chapter 1, membership of ICOM grew from just 1,000 in 1974 to around 180,000 in 2006.[11] This rise in the number of museums sector workers worldwide has led to moves towards the 'professionalisation' of museum staff, as well as greater specialisation and complexity within the workforce.[12] In 1965, ICOM recognised at least 11 distinct categories of museum professional, including 'museum curators, scientific laboratory personnel, restorers of works of art, conservation technicians, qualified persons ... recruited from the teaching profession' as well as technical personnel involved in 'audio-visual techniques, [exhibition] installation and presentation, lighting, climate conditioning, security, library techniques and documentation'.[13]

In addition, traditional curatorial duties such as collecting, collections management and registration work, conservation, research and the creation of displays and interpretation have become more strictly divided: in some museums they are assigned to staff with specialised functions, specific role profiles and job titles.[14] 'Curating' is still considered as a highly skilled, subject-specific profession and today many undergraduate and postgraduate training programmes specifically in curatorship have been established across the world, with options ranging from arts administration to curatorial practice in a range of subjects and pertaining to a variety of objects.[15]

The place of the museum curator

The changes in the nature of museum work and the tendency to place more emphasis on audience participation and the user experience has inevitably affected the traditional role of the scholar-curator. In general, the number of curators in museums has not risen at the same rate as for other museum staff in the last 50 years.[16] The proportion of curatorial staff in a museum varies according to the particular nature of a museum: the mission and aims of one organisation may encourage a greater emphasis on research and require greater numbers of subject-specialist curators to be employed. In other museums this may not be as much of a priority.

Curators still play an important, and vital, role in carrying out scholarly research and communicating understanding about historic objects, past lives and culture. Sometimes their role as guardians of culture and heritage is overlooked in favour of the museum sector's more visible outputs in exhibitions and programming. Such outputs would not be possible without the other functions curators perform in the museum relating to the collecting, preservation, management and research of objects. Curators must find ways to balance the safety, preservation and documentation of objects (which would most effectively be achieved by keeping them in dark stores, closed to the public) with the wish to provide public access for education and entertainment through study, display and handling.[17]

Curators of the future

Managing, caring for, and carrying out research into collection objects are vital aspects of curatorship today. A curator also needs to be pragmatic, flexible, diplomatic and possess a diverse range of other skills in public communication and learning; communication with colleagues, suppliers and stakeholders; project management and organisation; people management; financial management and commercial activity; and the use of technology and management of digital outputs. Many curators are active advocates of the value of their work in facilitating public engagement and learning and publicise their commitment to this.[18]

As noted throughout this book, museums have changed in the last 50 years: there is now an emphasis on the user, on participation, discovery, experiential and enquiry-based learning, and on relevancy and accessibility. With most museums now encouraging participation and engaging in dialogue with the public, the curator is no longer prioritised as the sole expert authority and is tasked with finding ways to present multiple perspectives and enable personal meaning-making in the displays and activities they deliver. A museum curator may be an historian but must also essentially be able to follow the contemporary developments, trends and issues of society, in order to connect the collections and work of the museum with wider humanity and the lives and concerns of audiences of today.[19]

An 'ability to work with computers' is an essential requirement for a career as a museum curator. Indeed, this skill is so commonplace today that job descriptions need not even mention it. Museum curators of the future require knowledge and expertise in digital technology and virtual platforms over and above this 'ability to work with computers'. The fact that museum activities and interpretation need not take place exclusively in the physical space of the museum, but instead in virtual spaces and very much in the public realm, has created a wealth of new opportunities for content and engagement. Museum curators will need to be receptive to technological developments, future trends, and ways of presenting and communicating in a virtual sense, adapting their outputs accordingly.

Many job descriptions for curatorial positions today also note the need for candidates to employ 'innovative, creative and dynamic' methods (often using the 'latest technology and digital media') through which to 'engage new audiences' and make museums more appealing. That museums are competing with one another, and with other organisations within the leisure and entertainment sector, means the curator must assist in delivering displays and activities that create entertaining experiences and appeal to many different people. This can be a motivating opportunity: curators are able to adapt and to offer considerable support to the modern museum's mission in widening participation, encouraging greater interactivity and raising visitor numbers. This unrelenting call to find original and inspiring ways to present information and engage the public can also be challenging, and occasionally overshadow the other curatorial function in areas such as research and the development of subject-specialist knowledge.

The value of museum objects and research

One way to achieve this wish to create 'challenging, exciting and unexpected encounters' is to re-examine one of the founding principles of many museums of the 18th and 19th centuries in collecting together and examining objects, and to consider the continued value of this activity in today's organisations. Museums can provide unique experiences, different to those of other entertainment providers: namely, real encounters with authentic historical objects. We must continue to unlock the value of objects in museum collections and ensure we are preserving them for a purpose: museum objects can contribute to intellectual stimulation and social learning, inspire curiosity and self-reflection, and facilitate contemplative, aesthetic or emotional experiences.

While embracing advances in technology and changing audience expectations, some attention and resources must also be directed to ensuring and maintaining experiential authenticity and accuracy in the museum. This requires a continued commitment to research.[20] The change in the position and duties of the curator from the early days of museums to today has impacted on this area of museum practice. The New Museology movement of the late 20th century added to this debate and in the last 40 years emphasis has been placed on audience-focussed and user-generated content, which has undoubtedly enriched museums and widened participation. In certain cases, this has also, however, shifted focus away from caring for and studying collections and resulted in the elimination of subject-specific staff and a suspicion of primary research, scholarly activity and academic partnerships, or assumptions that such activity can only bring limited (and not cost-effective) benefits. The challenges that museums face in securing and maintaining public funding add to these difficulties. Some museums no longer regard primary and object-based research as key to their core function and reduce the priority of this activity in the work of the organisation. In some museums, management staff can be hesitant to support projects that include the requirement for more academically focussed research, because of their concern that such activity can be of a long duration and produce few tangible or low-impact outcomes. In other museums, staff may not feel they have the skills and experience to engage in this perceived scholarly activity.

Frequently, the place of the expert curator and curatorial expertise within the museum is unclear, and the value of research to the quality of the visitor experience is not recognised.[21] There is a major risk that the loss of expertise surrounding primary research into collections and in partnership working with academic institutions will compromise the accuracy, authenticity and trustworthiness of a museum.[22] There is a further danger that collection objects may be considered of lesser value in performing the museum's functions, and be replaced with purely interactive, participatory and technological media. A more extreme outcome is that museums may find themselves producing and promoting low-quality products resulting from limited and superficial content development.

A museum is not a university or research centre but can produce research outputs that will support its public engagement activities and add to the value of the objects in its collections. Research conducted by museum staff and the public using collections can lead to the generation of new knowledge and material, original and creative interpretation, and a wide range of other outputs. Some museums were founded so that objects could be used in teaching or reference (natural history, archaeological or art collections perhaps most commonly): the pedagogical value of objects is proven, and collections-based and enquiry-based approaches to teaching can be strengthened by research activity.[23] Research can also broaden the appeal of museum objects to wider audiences by uncovering new information and stories of relevance to the lives of more diverse people or visitors previously unrepresented in mainstream history. Uncovering new information can also help museums to acknowledge and explore the often controversial and contested histories of the objects they care for.

The idea that a museum should develop a clear research policy was introduced in Chapter 6 (Generating concepts for displays and exhibitions); a Research Policy will set out a museum's commitment, vision and priorities for research over a short and longer-term period. It will state what research will be undertaken, by whom, over what time period, with what resources, and how this research is in keeping with, or will strengthen, the museum's mission and activities. A museum's work in this area will also be supported by actions that seek to build closer links with sources of knowledge and expertise outside of the organisation. This can include museum visitors, researchers, students, universities, independent industry partners and commercial partners. These contributors can offer different perspectives and add specialist knowledge and complementary skills to projects.

Every museum has something unique in their collections, and research is always possible, yet the attitude of different institutions to the role and value of research can vary considerably. Curatorial research must be at the heart of the museum, not carried out in isolation, but integrated with the museum's public outputs and its long-term development. Research should not be seen as a luxury addition to the activity of the museum, but instead part of its core work, informing (and being informed by) the plans and priorities of the museum for which it is conducted. A commitment to creating opportunities for research in a wide range of disciplines can only enhance the museum's strength as a relevant and active institution. Managing an active research programme, supporting staff research plans, and providing staff with time and resources to continue their research activities and develop their expertise are vital to this.

Notes

Introduction

1 E. Alexander and M. Alexander, *Museums in Motion*, 3rd edn, Lanham, Rowman and Littlefield, 2017, p.192.

2 A. George, *The Curator's Handbook*, London, Thames & Hudson, 2015, p.2.

3 J. Harrison, 'Ideas of Museums in the 1990s', in G. Gorsane (ed.), *Heritage, Museums and Galleries: An Introductory Reader*, London, Routledge, 2004, p.39.

4 For a useful introduction to this area of work, see G. Edson, 'Museum Management', in P. Boylan (ed.), *Running a Museum: A Practical Handbook*, Paris, ICOM, 2004, pp 147–60.

5 George, *The Curator's Handbook*, p.8.

1 What are museums?

1 ICOM, 'About ICOM', *ICOM* [website], n.d., http://umac.icom.museum/membership/about-icom/ (accessed 10 October 2018).

2 ICOM, 'Missions and Objectives', *ICOM* [website], 2016, https://icom.museum/en/about-us/missions-and-objectives/ (accessed 10 October 2018).

3 ICOM, 'Museum Definition', *ICOM* [website], 2018, https://icom.museum/en/activities/standards-guidelines/museum-definition/ (accessed 11 October 2018).

4 G. Lewis, 'The Role of Museums and the Professional Code of Ethics', in Boylan (ed.), *Running a Museum*, p.4.

5 A useful volume with definitions of major aspects of museum practice and theory is A. Desvallées and F. Mairesse, *Key Concepts of Museology*, Paris, Armand Colin, 2010.

6 M. Walhimer, *Museums 101*, London, Rowman and Littlefield, 2015, p.6.

7 Botanical gardens have been excluded from the following discussion, as distinct from the museum, though the first is usually named as the University of Pisa's physic garden, established in 1543 and used for study and teaching at the university.

8 V. León, *Uppity Women of Ancient Times*, Berkeley, Conari Press, 1995.

9 Lewis, 'The Role of Museums', p.1.

10 L. Woolley, *Excavations at Ur – A Record of Twelve Years' Work by Sir Leonard Woolley*, London, Ernest Benn Ltd, 1955; L. Woolley, *Ur "of the Chaldees": The Final Account, Excavations at Ur*, New York, Herbert Press, 1982.

11 J. Abt, 'The Origins of the Public Museum', in S. Macdonald (ed.), *A Companion to Museum Studies*, Malden, Blackwell Publishing, 2006, p.115.

12 Alexander and Alexander, *Museums in Motion*, p.3. Ptolemy Soter wished to emulate Alexander the Great, who had been taught by Aristotle.

13 Alexander and Alexander, *Museums in Motion*, p.4.

14 Abt, 'The Origins of the Public Museum', p.117.

15 Abt, 'The Origins of the Public Museum', p.117.

16 E. Schulz, 'Notes on the History of Collecting and of Museums', in S. Pearce (ed.), *Interpreting Objects and Collections*, London, Routledge, 1994, pp 175–87.

17 Abt, 'The Origins of the Public Museum', p.123.

18 Lewis, 'The Role of Museums', p.2.

19 Tradescant the elder had been 'Keeper of his Majesty's Gardens, Vines, and Silkworms'.

20 Thought to be a reference to Noah's Ark.

21 R.F. Ovenel, *The Ashmolean Museum, 1683–1894*, Oxford, Clarendon Press, 1986, pp 22ff.

22 Abt, 'The Origins of the Public Museum', p.125.

23 ICOM, 'Museum Definition', accessed 11 October 2018.

24 E. Miller, *That Noble Cabinet: A History of the British Museum*, Athens, Ohio University Press, 1974, pp 28–63.

25 For more on this and subsequent changes, see D. Cash, *Access to Museum Culture: The British Museum from 1753 to 1836*, British Museum Occasional Paper No.133, 2002, http://www.britishmuseum.org/research/publications/

research_publications_series/2002/access_to_museum_culture.aspx (accessed 11 October 2018).
26 Lewis, 'The Role of Museums', pp 3–4.
27 Lewis, 'The Role of Museums', pp 70–81.
28 A. Burton, *The Development of Museums in Victorian Britain and the Contribution of the Society of Arts*, The William Shipley Group for RSA History, Occasional Paper, No.16, 2010.
29 K. Hill, *Culture and Class in English Public Museums, 1850–1914*, Aldershot, Ashgate, 2005.
30 P. Boylan, 'The Museum Profession', in Macdonald (ed.), *A Companion to Museum Studies*, p.415; G. Dexter Lord, G. Quiang, A. Laishun and J. Jimenez (eds), *Museum Development in China*, Lanham, Rowman and Littlefield, 2019.
31 Boylan, 'The Museum Profession', p.415.
32 S. Knell (ed.), *Care of Collections*, London, Routledge, 2005, p.2.
33 Harrison, 'Ideas of Museums in the 1990s', p.42.
34 Useful guidelines for writing and using mission statements can be found in G. Anderson, *Museum Mission Statements: Building a Distinctive Identity*, Washington DC, American Association of Museums, 2000.
35 For more on the standards and ethics museums should comply with, see Lewis, 'The Role of Museums', pp 6–16.
36 Arts Council England, 'About Accreditation', *UK Museum Accreditation Scheme* [website], https://www.artscouncil.org.uk/accreditation-scheme/about-accreditation, (accessed 18 July 2019).
37 T. Ambrose and C. Paine, *Museum Basics*, 3rd edn, Abingdon, Routledge, 2006, p.14.
38 Ambrose and Paine, *Museum Basics*, p.6.
39 Harrison, 'Ideas of Museums in the 1990s', p.42.
40 M. Foley and G. McPherson, 'Museums as leisure', *International Journal of Heritage Studies*, vol.6, no.2, 2000, 161–74.
41 W. Boyd, 'Museum accountability: laws, rules, ethics and accreditation', *Curator: The Museum Journal*, vol.34, no.3, 1991, 165–77; G. Ashworth, *Heritage Planning: Conservation as the Management of Urban Change*, Groningen, Geo Pers, 1991, quoted in G. Graham, G. Ashworth and J. Tunbridge, 'The Uses and Abuses of Heritage', in G. Corsane (ed.), *Heritage, Museums and Galleries: An Introductory Reader*, London, Routledge, 2005, p.29.
42 Graham, Ashworth and Tunbridge, 'The Uses and Abuses of Heritage', p.29.
43 K. Hudson in M. Negri (ed.), *New Museums in Europe 1977–1983*, Milan, Mazzotta, 1984; E. Gurian, 'A blurring of the boundaries', *Curator: The Museum Journal*, vol.38, no.1, 1995, 31–7; S. Weil, *Rethinking the Museum and Other Meditations*, Washington DC, Smithsonian Institution Press, 1990, pp 55–6.
44 Harrison, 'Ideas of Museums in the 1990s', p.39.
45 Harrison, 'Ideas of Museums in the 1990s', p.39; see also D. Cameron, 'The museum, a temple or the forum', *Curator: The Museum Journal*, vol.14, no.1, 1971, pp 11–24.
46 Weil, *Rethinking the Museum and Other Meditations*, pp 55–6.
47 For more on this see P. Vergo (ed.), *The New Museology*, London, Reaktion Books, 1989.
48 Graham, Ashworth and Tunbridge, 'The Uses and Abuses of Heritage', p.29; B. Anderson, *Imagined Communities: Reflections on the Origin and Spread of Nationalism*, London, Verso, 1991, chapter 2.
49 For more on the social value of museums see A. Newman, 'Understanding the Social Impact of Museums, Galleries and Heritage through the Concept of Capital', in Corsane (ed.). *Heritage, Museums and Galleries*, pp 228–40.
50 Ambrose and Paine, *Museum Basics*, p.9.
51 Graham, Ashworth and Tunbridge, 'The Uses and Abuses of Heritage', p.29.
52 For more on the impact museums can have on tourism and a country's economy, see Graham, Ashworth and Tunbridge, 'The Uses and Abuses of Heritage', p.29; R. Prentice, 'Heritage: A Key Sector in the "New" Tourism', in Corsane (ed.). *Heritage, Museums and Galleries*, pp 243–56.

2 Collecting policies, composition and implementation

1 R. Phillips, 'The accumulator', *Archives of General Psychiatry*, vol.6, 1962, 474–7; J. Baudrillard, 'The System of Collecting', in J. Elsner and R. Cardinal (eds), *The Cultures of Collecting*, London, Reaktion Books, 1994, p.22; J. Simmons, *Things Great and Small: Collections Management Policies*, 2nd edn, Lanham, Rowman and Littlefield, 2018, p.61.
2 Baudrillard, 'The System of Collecting', p.8.
3 R.J. Lane, *Jean Baudrillard*, New York, Routledge, 2000, p.72.
4 S. Pearce, *On Collecting: An Investigation into Collecting in the European Tradition*, London, Routledge, 1995, p.16; R. Belk, M. Wallendorf, J. Sherry and M. Holbrook, 'Collecting in a Consumer Culture', *Highways and Buyways: Naturalistic Research from the Consumer Behavior Odyssey*, Provo, Association for Consumer Research, 1990, p.8.
5 Pearce, *On Collecting*, p.14.

6 Baudrillard, 'The System of Collecting', p.8.
7 S. Pearce, 'The Urge to Collect', in Pearce (ed.), *Interpreting Objects and Collections*, pp 157–9.
8 Baudrillard, 'The System of Collecting', p.16.
9 F. Baekeland, 'Psychological Aspects of Art Collecting', in Pearce (ed.), *Interpreting Objects and Collections*, p.215.
10 Baudrillard, 'The System of Collecting', p.7.
11 J. Elsner and R. Cardinal, 'Introduction', in, Elsner and Cardinal (eds), *The Cultures of Collecting*, p.3.
12 Baekeland, 'Psychological Aspects of Art Collecting', p.206.
13 L. Wacquant, 'Habitus', in J. Becket and Z. Milan (eds), *International Encyclopaedia of Economic Sociology*, London, Routledge, 2005, p.316.
14 B.S. Turner, *Status*, Milton Keynes, Open University Press, 1988, p.66; P. Bourdieu, 'Symbolic power', *Critique of Anthropology*, vol.13, 1979, 77–85.
15 J. Gaventa, 'Power after Lukes: an overview of theories of power since Lukes and their application to development', Brighton Participation Group, Institute of Development Studies [online article], 2003, https://www.powercube.net/wp-content/uploads/2009/11/power_after_lukes.pdf (accessed 13 October 2018).
16 Ambrose and Paine, *Museum Basics*, p.134.
17 S. Macdonald, 'Collecting Practices', in Macdonald (ed.), *A Companion to Museum Studies*, p.81.
18 Macdonald, 'Collecting Practices', p.81.
19 Baudrillard, 'The System of Collecting', p.7.
20 R. Belk, 'Collectors and Collecting', in Pearce (ed.), *Interpreting Objects and Collections*, pp 317–26; S. Pearce, 'Collecting Reconsidered', in Pearce (ed.), *Interpreting Objects and Collections*, pp 193–204.
21 'Collecting Methods', in D. Fleming, C. Paine and J. Rhodes (eds), *Social History in Museums*, London, HMSO, 1993, pp 176–208.
22 Macdonald, 'Collecting Practices', p.81.
23 E. Nicholson and E. Williams, 'Developing a working definition for the museum collection', *Inside Line*, Fall 2002, 1–4.
24 Alexander and Alexander, *Museums in Motion*, p.188.
25 Macdonald, 'Collecting Practices', p.81.
26 Ambrose and Paine, *Museum Basics*, p.140.
27 Simmons, *Things Great and Small*, pp 37–8.
28 M. Ware, *Museum Collecting Policies and Loan Agreements*, AIM Guidelines 14, Association of Independent Museums, 1988.
29 N. Merriman, 'Museum collections and sustainability', *Cultural Trends*, vol.17, no.1, 2008, 3–21, DOI: 10.1080/09548960801920278.
30 Macdonald, 'Collecting Practices', p.81.
31 T. Sola, 'Redefining Collecting', in S. Knell (ed.), *Museums and the Future of Collecting*, 2nd edn, Abingdon, Routledge, 2016, pp 187–96.
32 'Collecting Policies', in Fleming, Paine and Rhodes (eds), *Social History in Museums*, pp 171–5.
33 ICOM, 'ICOM Code of Ethics for Museums', *ICOM* [website], 2004, https://icom.museum/wp-content/uploads/2018/07/ICOM-code-En-web.pdf (accessed 12 December 2018). See Chapter 1 for further details on this organisation.
34 S. Hillhouse, *Collections Management: A Practical Guide*, Cambridge, Collections Trust, 2009, p.30; J. Nicks, 'Collections Management', in B. Lord, G. Dexter Lord and L. Martin (eds), *The Manual of Museum Planning: Sustainable Space, Facilities, and Operations*, 3rd edn, Lanham, AltaMira Press, 2012, pp 109–23; Lewis, 'The Role of Museums', p.7.
35 For some interesting case studies on this subject see N. Brodie and K. Walker Tubb, *Illicit Antiquities: The Theft of Culture and the Extinction of Archaeology*, London, Routledge, 2012.
36 For a useful guide to the key legal issues and concerns museums face see H. Kuruvilla, *A Legal Dictionary for Museums*, Lanham, Rowman and Littlefield, 2016.
37 ICOM, 'ICOM Code of Ethics for Museums'.
38 Some useful guides are P. Askerud and E. Clément, *Preventing the Illicit Traffic in Cultural Property: A Resource Handbook for the Implementation of the 1970 UNESCO Convention*, Paris, UNESCO, Division of Cultural Heritage, 1997; P. O'Keefe, *Commentary on the UNESCO 1970 Convention on Illicit Traffic*, Leicester, Institute of Art and Law, 2002.
39 UNESCO, *Convention on the Means of Prohibiting and Preventing the Illicit Import, Export and Transfer of Ownership of Cultural Property* [convention], 1970, http://www.unesco.org/new/en/culture/themes/illicit-trafficking-of-cultural-property/1970-convention/, (accessed 12 September 2019); UNIDROIT, *UNIDROIT Convention on Stolen or Illegally Exported Cultural Objects* [convention], 1995, https://www.unidroit.org/instruments/cultural-property/1995-convention (accessed 12 September 2019).
40 A. Fahy, 'Introduction', in A. Fahy (ed.), *Collections Management*, Abingdon, Routledge, 1994.
41 Lewis, 'The Role of Museums', p.13; L. Prott, 'Illicit Traffic', in Boylan (ed.), *Running a Museum*, pp 197–205. See also R. Thornes, *Protecting Cultural Objects Through International Documentation Standards*,

Santa Monica, The Getty Art History Information Programme, 1995.

42 In the UK, the Department for Culture Media and Sport, Cultural Property Unit, published due diligence guidelines relating to collecting and borrowing cultural material: Department for Culture, Media and Sport, Cultural Property Unit, *Combating Illicit Trade: Due Diligence Guidelines for Museums, Libraries and Archives on Collecting and Borrowing Cultural Material*, London, DCMS, 2005. The Museums Association in the UK also issues guidance, see Museums Association, 'Acquisition: Guidance on the Ethics and Practicalities of Acquisition', *Ethical Guidelines: Advice from the Museums Association Ethics Committee* [web resource], 2004, https://www.museumsassociation.org/download?id=11114, (accessed 18 July 2019).

43 J. Courtney (ed.), *The Legal Guide for Museum Professionals*, New York, Rowman and Littlefield, 2015, chapters 1–3.

44 Macdonald, 'Collecting Practices', p.81.

45 For more on this, see W. Logan and K. Reeves (eds), *Places of Pain and Shame: Dealing with 'Difficult' Heritage*, London, Routledge, 2009; J. Merryman, *Imperialism, Art, and Restitution*, New York, Cambridge University Press, 2006; J. Young and C. Buck (eds), *The Ethics of Cultural Appropriation*, New York, Wiley-Blackwell, 2009.

46 For more on this issue, see C. Wintle, 'Decolonising the museum: the case of the Imperial and Commonwealth Institutes', *Museum and Society*, vol.1, no.2, 2013, 185 201; R. Aldrich, 'Colonial Museums in a Postcolonial Europe', in D. Thomas (ed.), *Museums in Postcolonial Europe*, London, Routledge, 2010, pp 12–31; T. Barringer and T. Flynn (eds), *Colonialism and the Object: Empire, Material Culture and the Museum*, London, Routledge, 1998; J. MacKenzie, *Museums and Empire: Natural History, Human Cultures and Colonial Identities*, Manchester, Manchester University Press, 2009; S. Longair and J. McAleer (eds), *Curating Empire: Museums and the British Imperial Experience*, Manchester, Manchester University Press, 2012.

47 A. Lorde, 'The Master's Tools Will Never Dismantle the Master's House', in A. Lorde, *Sister Outsider: Essays and Speeches*, Trumansburg, Crossing Press, 2007, pp 110–14; S. Kassim, 'The museum will not be decolonised', *Media Diversified* [article], 2017, https://mediadiversified.org/2017/11/15/the-museum-will-not-be-decolonised/ (accessed 12 September 2019).

48 S. Vawda, 'Museums and the epistemology of injustice: from colonialism to decoloniality', *Museum International*, vol.71, no.1, 2019, 72–9.

49 C. Kreps, 'Changing the Rules of the Road: Postcolonialism and the New Ethics of Museum Anthropology', in J. Marstine (ed.), *The Routledge Companion to Museum Ethics: Redefining Ethics for the 21st-Century Museum*, New York, Routledge, 2011.

50 For more on this debate, see E. Barkan and R. Bush. *Claiming the Stones / Naming the Bones: Cultural Property and the Negotiation of National and Ethnic Identity*, Los Angeles, Getty, 2003; J. Cuno, *Whose Culture? The Promise of Museums and the Debate Over Antiquities*, Princeton, Princeton University Press, 2012; J. Greenfield, *The Return of Cultural Treasures*, 3rd edn, New York, Cambridge University Press, 2007; K. Fitz Gibbons (ed.), *Who Owns the Past? Cultural Policy, Cultural Property, and the Law*, New Brunswick, Rutgers University Press, 2005.

51 See also, A. Vrdoljak, *International Law, Museums and the Return of Cultural Objects*, New York, Cambridge University Press, 2006.

52 Knell (ed.), *Museums and the Future of Collecting*, p.87.

53 For more on this issue, see Cuno, *Whose Culture?*; Elsner and Cardinal (eds), *The Cultures of Collecting*, p.57.

54 C. Fforde, J. Hubert and P. Turnbull (eds), *The Dead and their Possessions: Repatriation in Principle, Policy and Practice*, London, Routledge, 2002.

55 For more on this issue, see V. Cassman, N. Odegaard and J. Powell (eds), *Human Remains: Guide for Museums and Academic Institutions*, Lanham, AltaMira Press, 2008.

56 See Section 47 of the Human Tissue Act 2004: The Government of the United Kingdom, 'Human Tissue Act 2004', *Guidance for Professionals* [website], https://www.hta.gov.uk/policies/human-tissue-act-2004 (accessed 9 September 2019).

57 See DCMS, 'Working Group on Human Remains, Report on Human Remains' [online report], 14 November 2003, https://webarchive.nationalarchives.gov.uk/+/http://www.culture.gov.uk/reference_library/publications/4553.aspx (accessed 9 September 2019); DCMS, 'Guidance for the Care of Human Remains in Museums' [online report], 2005, https://search.britishmuseum.org/pdf/DCMS%20Guide.pdf (accessed 9 September 2019); In addition, the display of human remains that are less than 100 years old in any UK museum requires a licence from the Human Tissue Authority.

58 Sola, 'Redefining Collecting', pp 187–96.

59 See also, S. Yerkovich, *A Practical Guide to Museum Ethics*, Lanham, Rowman and Littlefield, 2016; M. Malaro and I. DeAngelis, *A Legal Primer on Managing Museum Collections*, 3rd edn, Washington DC, Smithsonian Books, 2012; P. Davies (ed.), *Museums and the Disposals*

Debate, Edinburgh, MuseumsEtc, 2011; S. Weil (ed.), *A Deaccession Reader*, Washington DC, American Association of Museums, 1997.
60 Ambrose and Paine, *Museum Basics*, p.138.
61 L. Smith, 'Deaccessioning', *Registrars' Quarterly*, Winter, 1992, pp 1–2.
62 A famous example in the UK is Northampton Borough Council, which ordered the Northampton Museum and Art Gallery to sell a 4,000-year-old Egyptian Sekhemka limestone statue from its collection at Christie's auction house in 2014.
63 Museums Association, 'Code of Ethics for Museums', *Museums Association* [website] 2015, https://www.museumsassociation.org/download?id=1155827 (accessed 7 January 2019).
64 G. Lewis, 'Attitudes to Disposal from Museum Collections', in Fahy (ed.), *Collections Management*; G. Lewis, 'Deaccessioning and the ICOM Code of Ethics', *ICOM News*, vol.56, no.1, 2003; Simmons, *Things Great and Small*, p.63.
65 ICOM, 'ICOM Code of Ethics for Museums'.
66 Weil (ed.), *A Deaccession Reader*, p.100.
67 Simmons, *Things Great and Small*, p.64.
68 M. Malaro, 'Collection Management Policies', in Fahy (ed.), *Collections Management*.
69 Simmons, *Things Great and Small*, p.91.
70 T. Schlereth, 'Contemporary collecting for future recollecting', *The Museum Studies Journal*, vol.1, no.3, 1984, pp 23–30.

3 Researching and accessioning new collection objects

1 Simmons, *Things Great and Small*, p.46.
2 A. Roberts, 'Inventories and Documentation', in Boylan (ed.), *Running a Museum*, pp 31–2.
3 N. Ladkin, 'Collections Management' in Boylan (ed.), *Running a Museum*, p.20.
4 Simmons, *Things Great and Small*, p.47.
5 B. Miller and A. McKune, 'In a generous spirit: museums as donees: standards, best practice and ethical and legal responsibilities', *Museum*, vol.90, no.4, 2011, 50–52; R. Vreeland, 'Donation process and procedure outline', *Museum*, vol.90, no.4, 2011, 2–53.
6 Simmons, *Things Great and Small*, p.51.
7 Simmons, *Things Great and Small*, p.50.
8 Ware, *Museum Collecting Policies and Loan Agreements*.
9 For more on this see Chapter 2: Legal and ethical restrictions on collectoing and Collecting sensitive material.
10 Alexander and Alexander, *Museums in Motion*, p.199.
11 Alexander and Alexander, *Museums in Motion*, p.199.
12 D. Dudley and I. Wilkinson (eds), *Museum Registration Methods*, Washington DC, American Association of Museums, 1989, p.14.
13 Collections Trust, 'Object Entry Forms', *Collections Trust* [web resource], 2017, https://collectionstrust.org.uk/resource/object-entry-forms/ (accessed 30 January 2019); see also R. Buck and J. Gilmore (eds), *MRM5: Museum Registration Methods*, 5th edn, American Association of Museum Press, 2010; and Malaro and DeAngelis, *A Legal Primer on Managing Museum Collections*.
14 Simmons, *Things Great and Small*, p.46.
15 Simmons, *Things Great and Small*, p.45.
16 S.A. Holm, *Facts and Artefacts. How to Document a Museum Collection*, Cambridge, MDA, 1998, pp 10–12.
17 Roberts, 'Inventories and Documentation', p.33.
18 Holm, *Facts and Artefacts*, pp 13–17.
19 Ambrose and Paine, *Museum Basics*, p.145.
20 S.A. Holm, 'Exit Documentation', in Holm, *Facts and Artefacts*, pp 26–30; Collections Trust, 'Exit Forms', *Spectrum Related Resources* [web resource], 2017, https://collectionstrust.org.uk/resource/object-exit-forms/ (accessed 30 January 2019).
21 Holm, *Facts and Artefacts*, pp 26–30.

4 Classifying, recording and cataloguing objects

1 J. Simmons, 'Collections Care and Management: History, Theory, and Practice', in C. McCarthy (ed.), *International Handbook of Museum Studies: Museum Practice*, London, Wiley-Blackwell, 2015, pp 221–47.
2 For a useful overview of the main areas of collections management, see Lewis, 'The Role of Museums', pp 7–11.
3 S. Knell, 'Introduction, The Context of Collections Care', in Knell (ed.), *Care of Collections*.
4 Hillhouse, *Collections Management*, p.3; P. Johnson, 'Introduction to Collection Management and Development', in P. Johnson, *Fundamentals of Collection Development*, 2nd edn, Chicago, The American Library Association, 2018.
5 Hillhouse, *Collections Management*, p.3.
6 Boylan (ed.), *Running a Museum*, pp 17–18.
7 Malaro and DeAngelis, *A Legal Primer on Managing Museum Collections*, p.43.
8 Simmons, *Things Great and Small*, p.6.
9 All of the plans and procedures mentioned here are explored in more detail in Chapters 2–5.
10 In the UK for example, this includes the Treasure Act 1996, Data Protection Act 1998, Freedom of Information

Act 2000, Disability Act 1995, Equality Act 2010, Human Tissue Act 2004.
11 Hillhouse, *Collections Management*, p.16.
12 M.L. Anderson, 'A clear view: the case for museum transparency', *Museum*, vol.89, no.2, 2010, 48–53.
13 J. Gardner, 'From Idiosyncratic to Integrated Strategic Planning for Collections', in McCarthy (ed.), *International Handbook of Museum Studies*, pp 203–20.
14 Walhimer, *Museums 101*, p.135.
15 S. Stone, 'Documenting Collections', in J. Thompson (ed.), *Manual of Curatorship*, 2nd edn, Oxford, Butterworth-Heinemann, 1992, p.215; H. Ashby, G. McKenna and M. Stiff, *SPECTRUM Knowledge Standards for Cultural Information Management*, Cambridge, MDA, 2001.
16 Collections Trust, 'Introduction to Spectrum 5.0', *Spectrum* [website], September 2017, https://collectionstrust.org.uk/spectrum/spectrum-5/ accessed 13 February 2019.
17 Collections Trust, 'All Procedures', *Spectrum* [website], September 2017, https://collectionstrust.org.uk/spectrum/procedures/ (accessed 13 October 2019).
18 ICOM, 'ICOM Code of Ethics for Museums'.
19 A. Roberts, *Planning the Documentation of Museum Collections*, Cambridge, MDA, 1985; Simmons, 'Collections Care and Management', pp 221–47.
20 Stone, 'Documenting Collections', p.213.
21 Thornes, *Protecting Cultural Objects*, pp 10–20.
22 Stone, 'Documenting Collections', p.213.
23 H. Eriksen and I. Unger, *The Small Museums Cataloguing Manual*, Victoria, Museums Australia, 2009.
24 C. Gosden and Y. Marshall, 'The cultural biography of objects', *World Archaeology*, vol.31, no.2, 1999, 169–78; A. Appadurai, 'Introduction', in A. Appadurai (ed.), *The Social Life of Things: Commodities in Cultural Perspective*, Cambridge, Cambridge University Press, 1988, pp 3–63; I. Kopytoff, 'The Cultural Biography of Things: Commoditization as Process,' in Appadurai (ed.), *The Social Life of Things*, pp 64–91.
25 South Western Federation of Museums and Galleries, 'Developing a Collections Management Framework', *Collections Trust*, [website], 2015, https://collectionstrust.org.uk/resource/developing-a-collections-management-framework/ (accessed 20 February 2019).
26 Roberts, 'Inventories and Documentation', p.39.
27 Simmons, *Things Great and Small*, p.57.
28 For more on how digital technology has transformed museum practice, see P. Marty and K. Burton Jones, *Museum Informatics: People, Information, and Technology in Museums*, New York: Routledge, 2009, section 3.
29 Roberts, *Planning the Documentation of Museum Collections*, p.20; Roberts, 'Inventories and Documentation', pp 40–44.
30 Holm, *Facts and Artefacts*, p.37.
31 Roberts, 'Inventories and Documentation', pp 33–5.
32 S. Holm, *Guidelines for Constructing a Museum Object Name Thesaurus*, Cambridge, MDA, 1993.
33 E. Orna, *Build Yourself a Thesaurus: A Step by Step Guide*, Norwich, Running Angel, 1983.
34 Holm, *Facts and Artefacts*, pp 24–5.
35 South Western Federation of Museums and Galleries, 'Developing a Collections Management Framework'.

5 Handling, storing and preserving objects

1 See Chapter 1: What are museums?
2 Ambrose and Paine, *Museum Basics*, p.163; Knell, 'Introduction: The Context of Collections Care', p.1.
3 Further details on many of the aspects discussed in this chapter can be found in the sources cited in the endnotes. See also ICOM's recommendations for the care of collections in museums presented in its *Code of Ethics for Museums*, 2.18–2.24: ICOM, 'ICOM Code of Ethics for Museums'.
4 Ambrose and Paine, *Museum Basics*, p.163.
5 Hillhouse, *Collections Management*, p.49.
6 Getty Conservation Institute, 'Preventative Conservation', in Knell (ed.), *Care of Collections*, 2005, pp 83–7.
7 C. Caple, 'Introduction', in Capel (ed.) *Preventive Conservation in Museums*, London, Routledge, 2012; Getty Conservation Institute, 'Preventative Conservation', pp 83–7.
8 For more on strategy, planning and management of conservation in museums see S. Keene, *Managing Conservation in Museums*, Oxford, Butterworth-Heinemann, 1996.
9 S. Michalski, 'Care and Preservation of Collections', in Boylan (ed.), *Running a Museum*, pp 78–83.
10 Michalski, 'Care and Preservation of Collections', pp 78–83.
11 L. Bullock, 'Light as an Agent of Decay', in Caple (ed.), *Preventive Conservation in Museums*, II.5.
12 Michalski, 'Care and Preservation of Collections', pp 78–9.
13 See P. Wilson, 'The Clore Gallery for the Turner Collections at the Tate Gallery: Lighting Strategy and Practice', in Knell (ed.), *Care of Collections*, p.1.
14 Ambrose and Paine, *Museum Basics*, p.172.
15 H. Lloyd and K. Lithgow, 'Physical Agents of Deterioration: Dust and Dirt', in Caple (ed.), *Preventive*

Conservation in Museums, II; see also S. Norbert and P. Banks, 'Indoor Air Pollution: Effects on Cultural and Historic Materials', in Knell (ed.), *Care of Collections*, pp 135–46.

16 For more on this see S. Bradley and D. Thickett, 'The Pollution Problem in Perspective', in Caple, *Preventive Conservation in Museums*, II.4.

17 Simmons, *Things Great and Small*, p.114.

18 B. Powell and M. Richard, *Collection Care: An Illustrated Handbook for the Care and Handling of Cultural Objects*, Lanham, Rowman & Littlefield, 2016.

19 National Trust, *The National Trust Manual of Housekeeping*, rev. edn, London, National Trust, 2011.

20 S. Rydera and A. Mendez, *Designing and Planning Space with IPM in Mind – The Darwin Centre Phase Two*, Presented at 11th International Working Conference on Stored Product Protection, 2014.

21 For more on this see The Museum Pests Working Group (MP-WG), 'Monitoring', *Museum Pests* [website], 2019, https://museumpests.net/monitoring-introduction/ (accessed 8 May 2019); D. Pinniger, *Integrated Pest Management in Cultural Heritage*, London, Archetype Publications, 2015. Also see D. Pinniger, *Pest Management – A Practical Guide*, London, Collections Trust, 2008 and D. Pinniger, *Pests in Houses Great and Small*, London, English Heritage, 2018.

22 A useful tool to help in the identification of pests and devise a plan of action was developed by Birmingham Museums in partnership with the Collections Trust: A. Crossman and D. Pinniger, *What's Eating Your Collection* [website], 2015, http://www.whatseatingyourcollection.com/ (accessed 8 May 2019). Also see The Museum Pests Working Group (MP-WG), 'Identification', *Museum Pests* [website], 2019, https://museumpests.net/identification/ (accessed 8 May 2019).

23 For more on all of these solutions see The Museum Pests Working Group (MP-WG), 'Solutions', *Museum Pests* [website], 2019, https://museumpests.net/solutions/ (accessed 8 May 2019).

24 M. Linnie, 'Pest Control in Museums: The Use of Chemicals and Associated Health Problems', in Knell (ed.), *Care of Collections*, pp 234–9.

25 S. Michalski, 'Relative Humidity and Temperature Guidelines', in Caple (ed.), *Preventive Conservation in Museums*, II.6.

26 Knell, 'Introduction: The Context of Collections Care', p.7.

27 Alexander and Alexander, *Museums in Motion*, p.220.

28 S. Staniforth, 'Light and Environmental Control and Measurement in National Trust Houses', in Knell (ed.), *Care of Collections*, pp 177–222; see also M. Cassar, *Environmental Management Guidelines for Museums and Galleries*, London, MGC and Routledge, 1995.

29 E. Wylie and S. Brophy, *The Green Museum: A Primer on Environmental Practice*, Lanham, AltaMira Press, 2008.

30 Ambrose and Paine, *Museum Basics*, p.177.

31 Walhimer, *Museums 101*, p.132.

32 For more on this, see N. Stolow, *Conservation and Exhibitions: Packing, Transport, Storage and Environmental Considerations*, London, Butterworth-Heinemann, 1987 and R. Mervin and M.F. Mecklenburg, *Art in Transit: Handbook for Packing and Transporting Paintings*, Washington DC, National Gallery of Art, 1991.

33 G. Miles, 'Object Handling', in Caple (ed.), *Preventive Conservation in Museums*. II.1; Powell and Richard, *Collection Care: An Illustrated Handbook for the Care and Handling of Cultural Objects*, p.56.

34 For further guidance on such policies see Buck and Gilmore (eds), *MRM5: Museum Registration Methods*; Powell and Richard, *Collection Care: An Illustrated Handbook for the Care and Handling of Cultural Objects*; British Museum, *A Guide to the Storage, Exhibition and Handling of Antiquities, Ethnographia and Pictorial Art*, London, British Museum Publications, 1990. There are many online resources available that offer guidelines and toolkits in the area of object handling, packing and transport.

35 National Parks Service, 'How To Select Gloves: An Overview For Collections Staff', *National Parks Service, Conserve O Gram*, September 2010, No.1/12, https://www.nps.gov/museum/publications/conserveogram/01-12.pdf (accessed 9 April 2019).

36 F. Howie (ed.), *Safety in Museums and Galleries*, London, Butterworth-Heinemann, 1987.

37 For more on storage, see J. Hilberry and S. Weinberg, 'Museum Collections Storage', in Knell, (ed.), *Care of Collections*, pp 155–75; C. Caple, 'Conservation Skills: Preventive Conservation – Storage', in Caple (ed.), *Preventive Conservation in Museums*, III; Ladkin, 'Collections Management', pp 24–5; British Museum, *A Guide to the Storage, Exhibition and Handling of Antiquities, Ethnographia and Pictorial Art*.

38 Knell, 'Introduction: The Context of Collections Care', p.8.

39 G. Ellis Burcaw, *Introduction to Museum Work*, 3rd edn, Lanham, AltaMira Press, 1983, p.102.

40 Certain categories of object will benefit from specific storage conditions and guidance should be sought from the following: Simmons, *Things Great and Small*; B. Applebaum, *Guide to Environmental Protection*

of Collections, Madison, Sound View Press, 1991; K. Backmann, *Conservation Concerns: A Guide for Collectors and Curators*, Washington DC, Smithsonian Institution Press, 1992; National Trust, *The National Trust Manual of Housekeeping*.

41 Simmons, *Things Great and Small*, p.56.

42 Knell, 'Introduction: The Context of Collections Care', p.6.

43 For some guidance see P. O'Reilly and A. Lord, *Basic Condition Reporting: A Handbook*, New York, South East Registrars' Association, 1988; M. Clavir, 'Ethics and Theory in Preventive Conservation', in Caple (ed.), *Preventive Conservation in Museums*, III; D. Van Horn, H. Culligan and C. Midgett, *Basic Condition Reporting*, 4th edn, Southeastern Registrars Association, Lanham, Rowman and Littlefield, 2015.

44 Simmons, *Things Great and Small*, p.119.

45 Walhimer, *Museums 101*, p.135; Arts Council England, *Accreditation Guidance* [web resource], June 2014, https://www.artscouncil.org.uk/sites/default/files/download-file/FINAL_201406_GuidanceSection2_PrintFriendly.pdf (accessed 9 April 2019).

46 Ambrose and Paine, *Museum Basics*, p.191.

47 Knell, 'Introduction: The Context of Collections Care', p.5.

48 Ellis Burcaw, *Introduction to Museum Work*, p.102.

49 Knell, 'Introduction: The Context of Collections Care', p.5.

50 P. Cannon-Brookes, 'The Role of the Curator Scholar in Conservation', in Knell (ed.), *Care of Collections*, pp 47–50.

51 Malaro, 'Collection Management Policies', p.18. For more on risk management in museums, see R. Waller, *A Risk Model for Collection Preservation*, International Council of Museums, Committee for Conservation, Preprints of the 13th Triennial Meeting, Rio de Janeiro, 2002, pp 102–7. See also E. Merritt (ed.), *Covering Your Assets: Facilities and Risk Management in Museums*, American Association of Museums, 2005, pp 46–8; N. Gwinn and J. Wellheiser (eds), *Preparing for the Worst, Planning for the Best: Protecting our Cultural Heritage from Disaster*, München, Saur, 2005.

52 For more on this, see Merritt (ed.), *Covering Your Assets: Facilities and Risk Management in Museums*, pp 46–8; J. Ashley-Smith, 'Risk Analysis', in Caple (ed.), *Preventive Conservation in Museums*, III; J. Ashley-Smith, *Risk Assessment for Object Conservation*, London, Butterworth-Heinemann, 1999.

53 Simmons, *Things Great and Small*, p.119.

54 For more on this see D. Liston (ed.), *Museum Security and Protection: A Handbook for Cultural Heritage Institutions*, London, Routledge, 1993; Resource: The Council for Museums, Archives and Libraries, *Security in Museums, Archives and Libraries: A Practical Guide*, London, Resource, 2003; P. Jirásek, 'Museum Security, including Disaster Preparedness', in Boylan (ed.), *Running a Museum*, pp 177–96.

55 Jirásek, 'Museum Security, including Disaster Preparedness', p.177.

56 Ambrose and Paine, *Museum Basics*, p.199.

57 The need for securing these objects to walls should be carefully balanced with a consideration of what could happen in the event of a disaster when objects might need to be quickly removed.

58 Ambrose and Paine, *Museum Basics*, p.199.

59 For more on this, see S. Cackett, 'Disaster Planning' in Thompson (ed.), *Manual of Curatorship*, pp 487–90; see also J. Hunter, 'Museum Disaster Preparedness and Planning', in Caple (ed.), *Preventive Conservation in Museums*, III; I. Jenkins, *Disaster Planning and Preparedness*, London, British Library, 1987.

60 See also J. Hunter, 'Museum Disaster Preparedness Planning', pp 240–45; see also Jenkins, *Disaster Planning and Preparedness*; Jirásek, 'Museum Security, including Disaster Preparedness', pp 187–96.

61 Knell, 'Introduction: The Context of Collections Care', p.9.

62 Ambrose and Paine, *Museum Basics*, p.193.

63 E. Griffith, 'Liability and Risk Management for Museums', in Fahy (ed.), *Collections Management*, pp 277–83.

64 Simmons, *Things Great and Small*, p.121.

65 See P. Nauert and C. Black, *Fine Arts Insurance: A Handbook for Art Museums*, Washington DC, Association of Art Museum Directors, 1979.

66 Simmons, *Things Great and Small*, p.121.

67 Ambrose and Paine, *Museum Basics*, p.197.

68 Ladkin, 'Collections Management', p.27. For more detail on what to consider when purchasing insurance, see Malaro, 'Collection Management Policies', pp 20–21.

6 Displaying objects

1 K. Molineux, 'Permanent Collection Displays', in B. Lord and M. Piacente (eds), *Manual of Museum Exhibitions*, 2nd edn, Lanham, Rowman and Littlefield, 2014, p.121.

2 B. Lord, 'The Purpose of Museum Exhibitions', in Lord and Piacente (eds), *Manual of Museum Exhibitions*, p.7.

3 For more on high-profile museum redisplays, reinterpretation and evaluation, see H. Paddon, *Redisplaying Museum Collections: Contemporary Display*

and Interpretation in British Museums, Abingdon, Routledge, 2016.
4 Lord, 'The Purpose of Museum Exhibitions', p.8.
5 B. Hansen, *Great Exhibits! An Exhibit Planning and Construction Handbook for Small Museums*, Lanham, Rowman and Littlefield, 2017, pp 2–4.
6 Ellis Burcaw, *Introduction to Museum Work*, p.124.
7 Molineux, 'Permanent Collection Displays', pp 122–3; M. Belcher, *Exhibitions in Museums*, Washington DC, Smithsonian Institution Press, 2000, p.44. There are exceptions to this, particularly in the case of historic properties where the aim might be to recreate a defined moment in time and therefore the displays will not change in this way.
8 Y. Herreman, 'Display, Exhibits and Exhibitions', in Boylan (ed.), *Running a Museum*, p.92.
9 Belcher, *Exhibitions in Museums*, p.48.
10 Lord, 'The Purpose of Museum Exhibitions', p.8.
11 Ellis Burcaw, *Introduction to Museum Work*, p.144.
12 For more on organising this kind of exhibition, see F. Matassa, *Organising Exhibitions: A Handbook for Museums, Libraries and Archives*, London, Facet Publishing, 2014, part 9; Belcher, *Exhibitions in Museums*, pp 53–5.
13 Herreman, 'Display, Exhibits and Exhibitions', p.95.
14 Hansen, *Great Exhibits!*, p.1.
15 E. Bogle, *Museum Exhibition Planning and Design*, Lanham, AltaMira Press, 2013, p.88.
16 Walhimer, *Museums 101*, p.59.
17 For more on this collaborative process, see Paddon, *Redisplaying Museum Collections*, pp 38–46, 60–65; see also G. Black, *The Engaging Museum: Developing Museums for Visitor Involvement*, London, Routledge, 2012, p.255.
18 M. Hall, *On Display*, 2nd edn, London, Lund Humphries, 1992, pp 23–4.
19 Lord, 'The Purpose of Museum Exhibitions', p.9.
20 Hansen, *Great Exhibits!*, p.8.
21 Belcher, *Exhibitions in Museums*, chapter 4; Ambrose and Paine, *Museum Basics*, p.96.
22 B. Lord, 'Where Do Exhibition Ideas Come From?', in Lord and Piacente (eds), *Manual of Museum Exhibitions*, p.23.
23 Alexander and Alexander, *Museums in Motion*, p.242; Hansen, *Great Exhibits!*, pp 16–17.
24 Lord, 'Where Do Exhibition Ideas Come From?', p.23.
25 Paddon, *Redisplaying Museum Collections*, pp 38–46.
26 For more on project conceptualisation and development see Paddon, *Redisplaying Museum Collections*; Matassa, *Organising Exhibitions*, part 1.
27 L. Dillon Wright, 'Curatorship and Content Development', in Lord and Piacente (eds), *Manual of Museum Exhibitions*, p.269.
28 Alexander and Alexander, *Museums in Motion*, p.242.
29 Walhimer, *Museums 101*, p.60.
30 J. Summers, *Creating Exhibits That Engage*, Lanham, Rowman and Littlefield, 2018, p.118.
31 Molineux, 'Permanent Collection Displays', p.123.
32 B. Lord, G. Dexter Lord and L. Martin, *The Manual of Museum Planning: Sustainable Space, Facilities, and Operation*, 3rd edn, Lanham, AltaMira Press, 2012, p.117.
33 Walhimer, *Museums 101*, p.59; Belcher, *Exhibitions in Museums*, chapter 6.
34 Ambrose and Paine, *Museum Basics*, p.97.
35 Lord, 'The Purpose of Museum Exhibitions', p.15.
36 Molineux, 'Permanent Collection Displays', p.127.
37 Ambrose and Paine, *Museum Basics*, p.97.
38 Ellis Burcaw, *Introduction to Museum Work*, p.102.
39 Knell, 'Introduction: The Context of Collections Care, p.9.
40 For more on the Participatory Museum approach, see N. Simon, *The Participatory Museum* [online book], 2010, http://www.participatorymuseum.org/read/ (accessed 3 June 2019).
41 G. Velarde, *Designing Exhibitions: Museums, Heritage, Trade and World Fairs*, Aldershot: Ashgate, 2001, p.43.
42 T. Klobe, *Exhibitions: Concept, Planning and Design*, Chicago, University of Chicago Press, 2013, p.2.
43 Klobe, *Exhibitions*, p.4.
44 A. Ortony, D. Norman and W. Revelle, 'Affect and Proto-affect in Effective Functioning', in J. Fellous and M. Arbib (eds), *Who Needs Emotions? The Brain Meets the Robot*, Oxford, Oxford University Press, 2005.
45 For more on the practicalities of designing museum displays, see Summers, *Creating Exhibits That Engage*, chapter 10.
46 Klobe, *Exhibitions*, p.5.
47 Alexander and Alexander, *Museums in Motion*, p.244.
48 D. Dean, *Museum Exhibition: Theory and Practice*, Abingdon, Routledge, 1994, p.46.
49 Dean, *Museum Exhibition*, pp 51–2.
50 For more on the theory behind this approach, see T. Roppola, *Designing for the Museum Visitor Experience*, New York, Routledge, 2014, chapter 7; Belcher, *Exhibitions in Museums*, pp 108–13.
51 Hansen, *Great Exhibits!*, pp 32–3.
52 Dean, *Museum Exhibition*, pp 54–5.
53 E. Hooper-Greenhill, 'Studying Visitors', in Macdonald (ed.), *A Companion to Museum Studies*, pp 362–76.

54 R. Strohmaier, G. Sprung, A. Nischelwitze and S. Schadenbauer, 'Using visitor-flow visualization to improve visitor experience in museums and exhibitions', *MW2015: Museums and the Web 2015* [website], 15 January 2015, https://mw2015.museumsandtheweb.com/paper/enhancing-visitor-experience-and-fostering-museum-popularity-through-deep-insights-in-the-placement-of-exhibits-by-new-techniques-in-visitor-flow-visualization-in-space-and-time/ (accessed 12 August 2019).
55 Dean, *Museum Exhibition*, p.55.
56 Klobe, *Exhibitions*, p.7.
57 Dean, *Museum Exhibition*, p.148.
58 Hall, *On Display*, chapter 13.
59 Belcher, *Exhibitions in Museums*, pp 122–5.
60 Alexander and Alexander, *Museums in Motion*, p.244.
61 Klobe, *Exhibitions*, p.19.
62 Dean, *Museum Exhibition*, p.37.
63 Klobe, *Exhibitions*, p.10.
64 Belcher, *Exhibitions in Museums*, pp 125–7.
65 Klobe, *Exhibitions*, pp 15–17.
66 Bogle, *Museum Exhibition Planning and Design*, p.27; Hall, *On Display*, pp 42–4.
67 For more on how to develop an exhibition brief, see Summers, *Creating Exhibits That Engage*, chapter 5; Velarde, *Designing Exhibitions*, chapter 3; Belcher, *Exhibitions in Museums*, chapter 8.
68 For more on this see Bogle, *Museum Exhibition Planning and Design*, p.27; Hall, *On Display*, section 1.
69 Y. Tang and Y. Mayrand, 'Design', in Lord and Piacente (eds), *Manual of Museum Exhibitions*, p.295.
70 Tang and Mayrand, 'Design', p.296.
71 Ambrose and Paine, *Museum Basics*, p.110.
72 Walhimer, *Museums 101*, p.60.
73 For more on planning and organising an exhibition, see Matassa, *Organising Exhibitions*, parts 2–5; Summers, *Creating Exhibits That Engage*, chapter 3; Velarde, *Designing Exhibitions*, chapter 6; Belcher, *Exhibitions in Museums*, chapter 7; Herreman, 'Display, Exhibits and Exhibitions', pp 91–104.

7 Interpreting objects

1 Alexander and Alexander, *Museums in Motion*, p.277; G. Hein, *Learning in the Museum*, London, Routledge, 1998, p.149; for more on this see R. Mason, 'Museums, Galleries and Heritage', in Corsane (ed.), *Heritage, Museums and Galleries: An Introductory Reader*, pp 200–214; Herreman, 'Display, Exhibits and Exhibitions', p.93.
2 K. Ames, *Ideas and Images: Developing Interpretive History Exhibits*, Walnut Creek, AltaMira Press, 1999, p.314.
3 Lord, 'The Purpose of Museum Exhibitions', p.10.
4 Belcher, *Exhibitions in Museums*, p.147.
5 S. Pearce, 'Objects as Meaning' in Pearce (ed.), *Interpreting Objects and Collections*, pp 19–29.
6 J. Hoskins, 'Introduction', in *Biographical Objects How Things Tell the Stories of Peoples' Lives*, New York, Routledge, 1998; I. Hodder, 'The Contextual Analysis of Symbolic Meanings', in Pearce (ed.), *Interpreting Objects and Collections*, pp 12–13. For more on the agency of objects, see I. Hodder, 'The "Social" in Archaeological Theory: An Historical and Contemporary Perspective', in L. Meskell and R. Pruecel (eds), *A Companion to Social Archaeology*, Malden, Blackwell, 2003, p.29; J. Hoskins, 'Agency, Biography, and Objects', in C. Tilley, et al. (eds), *Handbook of Material Culture*, London, Sage Publications, 2006, p.79; A. Gell, *Art and Agency: An Anthropological Theory*, Oxford, Clarendon Press, 1998, p.95; C. Tilley, 'Ethnography and Material Culture', in P. Atkinson et al. (eds), *Handbook of Ethnography*, London, Sage Publications, 2001, p.260; C. Knappett, 'Animacy, Agency, and Personhood', in *Thinking through Material Culture: An Interdisciplinary Perspective*, Philadelphia, University of Pennsylvania Press, 2005, p.29
7 For more on this subject, see Appadurai (ed.), *The Social Life of Things*; Hoskins, *Biographical Objects*; N. Thomas, *Entangled Objects: Exchange, Material Culture, and Colonialism in the Pacific*, Cambridge, Harvard University Press, 1991.
8 For more ways to consider material culture and museum objects, see S. Pearce, 'Thinking About Things', in Pearce (ed.), *Interpreting Objects and Collections*, pp 125–32.
9 R. Bachelor, 'Not Looking at Kettles', in Pearce (ed.), *Interpreting Objects and Collections*, pp 139–43; E. Hooper-Greenhill, *Learning and Teaching with Objects: A Practical Skills Based Approach*, Leicester, Department of Museum Studies, University of Leicester, 1988.
10 Some useful case studies illustrating the power objects can have and some innovative approaches to their interpretation in museums, drawing on object biographies, can be found in S. Dudley, *Museum Materialities: Objects, Engagements, Interpretations*, London, Routledge, 2013.
11 K. Arnold, *Cabinets for the Curious*, Aldershot, Ashgate, 2006; see also L. Bedford, *The Art of Museum Exhibitions: How Story and Imagination Create Aesthetic Experiences*, London, Routledge, 2016.

12 Ellis Burcaw, *Introduction to Museum Work*, p.129; Summers, *Creating Exhibits That Engage*, p.55.
13 For more on communication objectives see M. Piacente, 'Interpretive Planning', in Lord and Piacente (eds), *Manual of Museum Exhibitions*, pp 260–61.
14 Piacente, 'Interpretive Planning', p.251.
15 Piacente, 'Interpretive Planning', pp 252–3.
16 Belcher, *Exhibitions in Museums*, p.157; Summers, *Creating Exhibits That Engage*, p.54.
17 Summers, *Creating Exhibits That Engage*, p.55.
18 For more on creating interpretive plans, see Summers, *Creating Exhibits That Engage*, pp 56–61.
19 Dillon Wright, 'Curatorship and Content Development', p.269.
20 F. Tilden, *Interpreting Our Heritage*, 4th edn, Chapel Hill, University of North Carolina Press, 2008, p.9 (first published 1957).
21 Lord, 'The Purpose of Museum Exhibitions', p.13.
22 Belcher, *Exhibitions in Museums*, p.155.
23 Ellis Burcaw, *Introduction to Museum Work*, p.125.
24 Hall, *On Display*, p.47.
25 B. Serrell, 'Paying attention: the duration and allocation of visitors' time in museum exhibitions', *Curator: The Museum Journal*, vol.40, no.2, 1997, 108–25; Hein, *Learning in the Museum*, p.67; P. McManus, 'Oh, yes, they do: how museum visitors read labels and interact with exhibit texts', *Curator: The Museum Journal*, vol.32, no.3, 1989, 174–89.
26 Piacente, 'Interpretive Planning', p.256. Storytelling and narrative in this way can be a useful organising structure for new knowledge, see J. Falk and L. Dierking, *Learning from Museums: Visitor Experiences and the Making of Meaning*, Lanham, AltaMira Press, 2000.
27 B. Serrell, *Exhibit Labels: An Interpretive Approach*, Walnut Creek, AltaMira Press, 1996, p.7.
28 Piacente, 'Interpretive Planning', p.257.
29 Piacente, 'Interpretive Planning', pp 257–8.
30 Serrell, *Exhibit Labels*, p.163.
31 See also C. Sjoberg, 'Addressing Learning Styles in the Interpretive Plan', in Lord and Piacente (eds), *Manual of Museum Exhibitions*, p.253; Belcher, *Exhibitions in Museums*, p.153.
32 K. McLean, *Planning for People in Exhibitions*, Washington DC, Association of Science-Technology Centers, 1993, pp 103–12.
33 Alexander and Alexander, *Museums in Motion*, p.236.
34 Serrell, *Exhibit Labels*, p.19.
35 McLean, *Planning for People in Exhibitions*, pp 103–12; Ambrose and Paine, *Museum Basics*, p.78.
36 Alexander and Alexander, *Museums in Motion*, p.263.
37 L. Ferguson, C. MacLulich and L. Ravelli, *Meanings and Messages: Language Guidelines for Museum Exhibitions*, Sydney, Australian Museum, 1995, p.4; Alexander and Alexander, *Museums in Motion*, p.248; Belcher, *Exhibitions in Museums*, p.156.
38 See, for example, J. Falk, 'The use of time as a measure of visitor behaviour and exhibit effectiveness', *Roundtable Reports: The Journal of Museum Education*, vol.7, no.4, 1982, 10–13; McManus, 'Oh, yes, they do: how museum visitors read labels and interact with exhibit texts', 174–89; E. Hooper-Greenhill, *Museums and their Visitors*, London, Routledge, 2012, pp 136ff; Serrell, 'Paying attention', 108–25.
39 C. Screven, 'Motivating visitors to read labels', *ILVS Review: A Journal of Visitor Behaviour*, vol.2, no.2, 1992, 183–211; D. Samson, 'Reading Strategies Used by Exhibition Visitors', in A. Blais (ed.), *Text in the Exhibition Medium*, Quebec City, Musée de la civilisation, 1995; Summers, *Creating Exhibits That Engage*, pp 62–6.
40 S. Bitgood, 'The ABCs of label design', *Visitor Studies: Theory, Research and Practice*, vol.3, no.1, 1991, pp 115–29.
41 Summers, *Creating Exhibits That Engage*, pp 69–71.
42 For more on possible hierarchies, structure and word counts see Belcher, *Exhibitions in Museums*, pp 167–8; Dillon Wright, 'Curatorship and Content Development', pp 277–9; Tang and Mayrand, 'Design', pp 316–18.
43 Dillon Wright, 'Curatorship and Content Development', p.277.
44 S. Bitgood, 'Practical Guidelines for Developing Interpretive Labels', *Visitor Behaviour*, Fall, 1996, 4–15.
45 Dean, *Museum Exhibition*, chapter 7; Bogle, *Museum Exhibition Planning and Design*, pp 173–88; Australian Museum, *Learning Resources*, 'Writing Text and Labels', https://australianmuseum.net.au/learn/teachers/learning/writing-text-and-labels/ 2019, (accessed 7 June 2019); The J. Paul Getty Museum, *Complete Guide*, 'Complete guide to adult audience interpretive materials: gallery texts and graphics', https://www.getty.edu/education/museum_educators/downloads/aaim_completeguide.pdf, 2011 (accessed 7 June 2019); V&A, *Gallery Text at the V&A: A Ten Point Guide* [online resource], 2009, http://media.vam.ac.uk/media/documents/legacy_documents/file_upload/10808_file.pdf (accessed 7 June 2019); B. Punt, S. Stern and S. Ratcliffe, *Doing It Right: A Workbook for Improving Exhibit Labels*, Brooklyn, The Museum, 1989.
46 McLean, *Planning for People in Exhibitions*, pp 103–12; Punt, Stern and Ratcliffe, *Doing it Right: A Workbook*

for Improving Exhibit Labels, p.32; Dillon Wright, 'Curatorship and Content Development', p.280; Hall, *On Display*, chapter 16; Hansen, *Great Exhibits!*, pp 46–8; Serrell, *Exhibit Labels*, chapter 19; Belcher, *Exhibitions in Museums*, pp 160–65.

47 Serrell, *Exhibit Labels*, p.49.

48 Alexander and Alexander, *Museums in Motion*, p.248; Ferguson, MacLulich and Ravelli, *Meanings and Messages*, p.65.

49 McLean, *Planning for People in Exhibitions*, p.103–12; Serrell, *Exhibit Labels*, p.234; Hansen, *Great Exhibits!*, pp 42–4; For more on graphics and models see Belcher, *Exhibitions in Museums*, chapter 10.

50 Dillon Wright, 'Curatorship and Content Development', p.283.

51 Formulae and tools available to calculate the readability of text in this way include the Gunning Fog Index, the Fry readability graph, the McLaughlin 'SMOG' readability formula, and the Flesch–Kincaid readability tests. See Belcher, *Exhibitions in Museums*, pp 165–6.

52 Serrell, *Exhibit Labels*, chapter 6.

53 For more on this see Serrell, *Exhibit Labels*, chapter 6.

54 McLean, *Planning For People in Exhibitions*, p.87.

55 Bitgood, 'The ABCs of label design', 115–29.

56 E. Hooper-Greenhill (ed.), *The Educational Role of the Museum*, 2nd edn, New York, Routledge, 1999, p.12; Falk and Dierking, *Learning from Museums*, p.131; C. Stainton, 'Voice and Images: Making Connections Between Identity and Art', in G. Leinhardt, K. Crowley and K. Knutson (eds), *Learning Conversations in Museums*, Mahwah, Erlbaum Associates, 2002.

57 For more on creating labels using these approaches see Serrell, *Exhibit Labels*, sections II and III.

58 Hall, *On Display*, p.100.

59 Serrell, *Exhibit Labels*, p.208.

60 Molineux, 'Permanent Collection Displays', p.130.

61 For a longer discussion on these techniques, see N. Blankenberg, 'Virtual Experiences', in Lord and Piacente (eds), *Manual of Museum Exhibitions*, pp 149–62; and H. Din and P. Hecht, *The Digital Museum: A Think Guide*, Washington DC, American Association of Museums, 2007; L. Tallom and K. Walker (eds), *Digital Technologies and the Museum Experience*, Lanham, AltaMira Press, 2008.

62 Belcher, *Exhibitions in Museums*, pp 141–5.

63 Alexander and Alexander, *Museums in Motion*, p.249.

64 Lord, 'The Purpose of Museum Exhibitions', p.15.

65 Molineux, 'Permanent Collection Displays', p.130.

8 Museum audiences

1 Alexander and Alexander, *Museums in Motion*, p.274.

2 S. Weil, 'From being about something to being for somebody: the ongoing transformation of the American museum', *Daedalus*, vol.128, no.3, 1999, 229–58.

3 See Hooper-Greenhill, *Museums and their Visitors*, pp 58–61.

4 J. Falk and L. Dierking, *The Museum Experience Revisited*, Walnut Creek, Left Coast Press, 2013.

5 See Hein, *Learning in the Museum*.

6 Dean, *Museum Exhibition*, p.25.

7 Lord, 'The Purpose of Museum Exhibitions', p.10.

8 J. Dodd and R. Sandell, *Building Bridges: Guidance for Museums and Galleries on Developing New Audiences*, London, Museums & Galleries Commission, 1998, p.5.

9 Lord, 'The Purpose of Museum Exhibitions', p.10.

10 Ellis Burcaw, *Introduction to Museum Work*, p.144.

11 Ellis Burcaw, *Introduction to Museum Work*, p.158.

12 E. Hooper-Greenhill, 'The Characteristics and Significance of Learning in Museums', in E. Hooper-Greenhill, *Museums and Education: Purpose, Pedagogy, Performance*, London, Routledge, 2010, chapter 10.

13 Z. Collins (ed.), *Museums, Adults and the Humanities: A Guide for Educational Programming*, Washington DC, American Association of Museums, 1984, p.93.

14 Ambrose and Paine, *Museum Basics*, p.46.

15 Sjoberg, 'Addressing Learning Styles in the Interpretive Plan', pp 253; for more on the three domains of learning as devised by American educational psychologists in the 1950s led by Benjamin Bloom, see B. Bloom, *A Taxonomy for Learning, Teaching, and Assessing: A Revision of Bloom's Taxonomy of Educational Objectives*, New York, Longman, 2001.

16 C. Brüninghaus-Knubel, 'Museum Education in the Context of Museum Functions', in Boylan (ed.), *Running a Museum*, pp 124–32.

17 H. Moffat and V. Woollard (eds), *Museum and Gallery Education: A Manual of Good Practice*, Walnut Creek, AltaMira Press, 2004, chapter 2; Brüninghaus-Knubel, 'Museum Education in the Context of Museum Functions', pp 120–21.

18 Ambrose and Paine, *Museum Basics*, p.48.

19 Ellis Burcaw, *Introduction to Museum Work*, p.121.

20 Bedford, *The Art of Museum Exhibitions*, p.25, p.38.

21 See J. Watson, 'Psychology as the behaviorist views it', *Psychological Review*, vol.20, no.2, 1913, 158–77; I. Pavlov, *Lectures on Conditioned Reflexes: Twenty-Five Years of Objective Study of the High Nervous Activity (Behavior) of Animals*, trans.by W. Horsley Gantt, New

York, International, 1928; B. Skinner, *Science and Human Behavior*, New York, Macmillan, 1953.

22 See J. Piaget, *Origins of Intelligence in the Child*, London, Routledge and Kegan Paul, 1936; J. Piaget, *The Psychology of Intelligence*, London, Routledge and Kegan Paul, 1950; L.S. Vygotsky, *Mind in Society: The Development of Higher Psychological Processes*, Cambridge, Harvard University Press, 1978 (original manuscripts 1930–34); J. Dewey, *Democracy and Education*, Milton Keynes, Simon and Brown, 2011 (original work published 1916).

23 See E. Hooper-Greenhill, *Museums and the Interpretation of Visual Culture*, London, Routledge, 2008.

24 See Hein, *Learning in the Museum*.

25 D. Kolb, *Experiential Learning Experience as the Source of Learning and Development*, Englewood Cliffs, Prentice Hall, 2003 (original work published 1984); Dewey, *Democracy and Education*, pp 217–18.

26 For more on this approach in museums see Roppola, *Designing for the Museum Visitor Experience*, chapter 3.

27 J. Bruner, 'The act of discovery', *Harvard Educational Review*, vol.31, no.1, 1961, 21–32; see Vygotsky, *Mind in Society*.

28 J. Moran, 'Curiosity is an inextinguishable creative spark', *Times Higher Education* [online article], 2017: https://www.timeshighereducation.com/comment/curiosity-is-an-inextinguishable-creative-spark (accessed 26 August 2019); M. Stenger, 'Why curiosity enhances learning', *Edutopia* [online article], 2014, https://www.edutopia.org/blog/why-curiosity-enhances-learning-marianne-stenger (accessed 26 August 2019); M. Gruber, B. Gelma and C. Ranganath, 'States of curiosity modulate hippocampus-dependent learning via the dopaminergic circuit', *Neuron*, vol.84, no.2, 2014, 486–96.

29 See Falk and Dierking, *Learning from Museums*.

30 Vygotsky, *Mind in Society*; J. MacDermott, (ed.), *The Philosophy of John Dewey*, Chicago, University of Chicago Press, 1973; J. Lave and E. Wenger, *Situated Learning: Legitimate Peripheral Participation*, Cambridge, Cambridge University Press, 1991.

31 H. Gardner *Intelligence Reframed: Multiple Intelligences for the 21st Century*, New York, Basic Books, 1999.

32 Ambrose and Paine, *Museum Basics*, p.48.

33 Gardner, *Intelligence Reframed*, pp 169–72; H. Gardner, *The Unschooled Mind*, New York, Basic Books, 1991, p.245; J. Davis, *The MUSE Book*, Cambridge, President and Fellows of Harvard College/Harvard Project Zero, 1996.

34 Klobe, *Exhibitions*, pp 51–2; a useful table of examples of potential interpretation techniques mapping to Gardner's principles can be found in Sjoberg, 'Addressing Learning Styles in the Interpretive Plan', p.254; Piacente, 'Interpretive Planning', p.261.

35 Ellis Burcaw, *Introduction to Museum Work*, p.121.

36 C. Scott (ed.), *Evaluation and Visitor Research in Museums: Towards 2000*, Sydney, Powerhouse Publishing, 1996.

37 V. Woollard, 'Caring for the Visitor', in Boylan (ed.), *Running a Museum*, p.109.

38 M. Hood, 'Audience Research Tells Us Why Visitors Come to Museums – and Why they Don't', in Scott (ed.), *Evaluation and Visitor Research in Museums*, pp 3–10.

39 Ambrose and Paine, *Museum Basics*, p.38.

40 Woollard, 'Caring for the Visitor', p.111.

41 Punt, Stern and Ratcliffe, *Doing It Right: A Workbook for Improving Exhibit Labels*.

42 See also E. Hooper-Greenhill, *Museums and Interpretive Communities*, Sydney, Australian Museum Audience Research Centre, 1999.

43 See also Roppola, *Designing for the Museum Visitor Experience*, chapter 5.

44 M. Hood, 'Staying away – why people choose not to visit museums', *Museum News*, vol.61, no.4, 1983, 50–57.

45 A. Pekarik, Z. Doering and D. Karns, 'Exploring satisfying experiences in museums', *Curator: The Museum Journal*, vol.42, no.2, 1999, 152–73; see also T. Moussouri and G. Roussos, 'Examining the effect of visitor motivation on visit strategies using mobile computer technologies', *Visitor Studies*, vol.16, no.1, 2013, 21–38.

46 Another interesting volume on this subject is S. Wilkening and J. Chung, *Life Stages of the Museum Visitor: Building Engagement Over a Lifetime*, Washington DC, AAM Press, 2009.

47 J. Falk, *Identity and Museum Visitor Experience*, Walnut Creek, Left Coast Press, 2009.

48 N. Bond and J.H. Falk, 'Who am I? And why am I here (and not there)? The role of identity in shaping tourist visit motivations', *International Journal of Tourism Research*, vol.15, no.15, 2012, 430–42.

49 For examples, see Serrell, *Exhibit Labels*, chapter 5.

50 Ambrose and Paine, *Museum Basics*, p.112; Paddon, *Redisplaying Museum Collections*, pp 67–73.

51 Hansen, *Great Exhibits!*, p.56.

52 G. Lord, 'Measuring Success', in Lord and Piacente, *Manual of Museum Exhibitions*, pp 39–44.

53 Lord, 'Measuring Success', pp 39–44; Museums Association, *Public Perceptions of – and Attitudes to*

– *the Purposes of Museums in Society* [online report], 2013, https://www.museumsassociation.org/download?id=954916 (accessed 22 August 2019).

54 H. Fry, S. Ketteridge and S. Marshall (eds), *A Handbook for Teaching and Learning in Higher Education*, 3rd edn, London, Kogan Page, 2003.

55 N. Blankenberg, 'Participatory Exhibitions', in Lord and Piacente (eds), *Manual of Museum Exhibitions*, p.166; H. Jenkins, K. Clinton, R. Purushotma, A.J. Robison and M. Weigel, 'Confronting the Challenge of Participatory Culture: Media Education for the 21st Century', *MacArthur*, 2009 [digital version], https://www.macfound.org/media/article_pdfs/JENKINS_WHITE_PAPER.PDF (accessed 29 August 2019).

56 Harrison, 'Ideas of Museums in the 1990s', p.39; Alexander and Alexander, *Museums in Motion*, p.10.

57 Lord, 'The Purpose of Museum Exhibitions', p.14.

58 For a useful guide on how to adopt this kind of approach, see Black, *The Engaging Museum*.

59 See also Simon, *The Participatory Museum*.

60 Blankenberg, 'Participatory Exhibitions', p.171.

61 B. Pitman, 'Muses, museums, and memories', *Daedalus*, vol.128, no.3, 1999, 1–31.

62 Collections Trust, 'Collections Management', *Collections Trust* [web resource], https://collectionstrust.org.uk/collections-management/ (accessed 13 February 2019).

9 The curator today and conclusions

1 D. Stam, 'The Informed Muse', in Corsane (ed.), *Heritage, Museums and Galleries: An Introductory Reader*, pp 56–9.

2 Harrison, 'Ideas of Museums in the 1990s', pp 160–76; Hooper-Greenhill, *Museums and Education*, p.27; W. Griswold, *Cultures and Societies in a Changing World*, 4th edn, Thousand Oaks, Sage Publications, 2013; see also, T. Bennett, *The Birth of the Museum: History, Theory, Politics*, London, Routledge, 1995.

3 I. Karp, C. Kreamer and S. Lavine (eds), *Museums and Communities: The Politics of Public Culture*, Washington DC, Smithsonian Institution Press, 1992; S. Weil, *Making Museums Matter*, Washington DC, Smithsonian Institution Press, 2002; Simon, *The Participatory Museum*; T. Satwicz and K. Morrissey, 'Public Curation: From Trend to Research-based Practice', in B. Adair, B. Filene and L. Koloski (eds), *Letting Go? Sharing Historical Authority in a User-Generated World*, Philadelphia, Pew Center for Arts and Heritage, 2011; Desvallées and Mairesse, *Key Concepts of Museology*; K. Message, *New Museums and the Making of Culture*, Oxford, Berg, 2006.

4 Cameron, 'The museum, a temple or the forum', p.23.

5 K. Hudson, *Museums for the 1980s: A Survey of World Trends*, Paris, UNESCO/Macmillan, 1977.

6 S. Weil (ed.), 'The Multiple Crises in our Museums', in S. Weil (ed.), *Beauty and the Beasts: On Museums, Art, the Law, and the Market*, Washington DC, Smithsonian Institute, 1990.

7 M. Ross, 'Interpreting the new museology', *Museum and Society*, vol.2, no.2, 84–103.

8 Black, *The Engaging Museum*, p.145; C. Kreps, 'Indigenous Curation, Museums, and Intangible Cultural Heritage', in L. Smith and N. Akagawa (eds), *Intangible Heritage: The Practices and Politics of Safeguarding*, 2nd edn, Abingdon, Routledge, 2018, pp 193–208; R. Sandell, *Museums, Prejudice and the Reframing of Difference*, London, Routledge, 2007.

9 R. Janes, *Museums in a Troubled World: Renewal, Irrelevance or Collapse?*, London, Routledge, 2012; R. Harrison, *Heritage: Critical Approaches*, London, Routledge, 2012.

10 Boylan, 'The Museum Profession', p.418.

11 Boylan, 'The Museum Profession', p.415.

12 Alexander and Alexander, *Museums in Motion*, p.306.

13 International Council of Museums Conference New York (City) and International Council of Museums, *Papers from the Seventh General Conference of ICOM*, Metropolitan Museum, New York, 1965; see also J. Teather, *Professional Directions for Museum Work in Canada*, Ottawa, Canadian Museums Association, 1978.

14 Boylan, 'The Museum Profession', p.415. A useful overview of the museum profession can be found in J. Glaser and A. Zenetou, *Museums: A Place to Work*, London, Routledge, 1996.

15 Arts Council England and BOP Consulting, *Character Matters: Attitudes, Behaviours and Skills in the UK Museum Workforce* [online report], 2016, https://www.artscouncil.org.uk/sites/default/files/download-file/ACE_Museums_Workforce_ABS_BOP_Final_Report.pdf (accessed 1 September 2019).

16 In some cases, in UK museums levels have not risen at all and have instead fallen. In 2006 it was estimated that around 12 per cent of the UK's museum workforce were curators: Boylan, 'The Museum Profession', p.420.

17 Lord, 'The Purpose of Museum Exhibitions', p.9.

18 See, for example, N. Cossons, 'Scholarship or Self-Indulgence?', in G. Kavanagh (ed.), *Museum Provision and Professionalism*, London, Routledge, 1994; W. McGillivray, 'Museum research: axiom or oxymoron', *Muse*, vol.9, no.2, 1991, 62–6; C. Mayer, 'The contemporary curator – endangered species or brave new profession', *Muse*,

Summer/Autumn, 1991, 34–8; R. Strong, 'Scholar or salesman? The curator of the future', *Muse*, vol.6, no.2, 1988, 16–20.

19 George, *The Curator's Handbook*, p.310.

20 S. Knell, 'The shape of things to come: museums in the technological landscape', *Museum and Society*, vol.1, no.3, 2003.

21 Black, *The Engaging Museum*, p.65; C. Lang, J. Reeve and V. Woollard (eds), *The Responsive Museum: Working with Audiences in the Twenty-First Century*, London, Routledge, 2016.

22 See N. MacGregor in Culture, Media and Sport Committee, *Oral Evidence: Countries of Culture*, HC 864, Questions 127–85 [online], 2016. available at: http://data.parliament.uk/writtenevidence/committeeevidence.svc/evidencedocument/culture-media-and-sport-committee/countries-of-culture/oral/32902.html (accessed 10 May 2018).

23 H. Chatterjee, 'Object-based learning in higher education: the pedagogical power of museums', *University Museums and Collections Journal*, vol.3, 2010, 179–81; R. Duhs, 'Learning from university museums and collections in higher education: University College London (UCL)', *University Museums and Collections Journal*, vol.3, 183–6; H. Chatterjee, 'Staying essential: articulating the value of object based learning', *University Museums and Collections Journal*, vol.2, 2007, 121–5.

Bibliography

Abt, J., 'The Origins of the Public Museum', in S. Macdonald (ed.), *A Companion to Museum Studies*, Malden, Blackwell Publishing, 2006

Adair, B., Filene, B., and Koloski, L. (eds), *Letting Go? Sharing Historical Authority in a User-Generated World*, Philadelphia, Pew Center for Arts and Heritage, 2011

Aldrich, R., 'Colonial Museums in a Postcolonial Europe', in D. Thomas (ed.), *Museums in Postcolonial Europe*, London, Routledge, 2010

Alexander, E., and Alexander, M., *Museums in Motion*, 3rd edn, Lanham, Rowman and Littlefield, 2017

Ambrose, T., and Paine, C., *Museum Basics*, 3rd edn, Abingdon, Routledge, 2006

Ames, K., *Ideas and Images: Developing Interpretive History Exhibits*, Walnut Creek, AltaMira Press, 1999

Anderson, B., *Imagined Communities: Reflections on the Origin and Spread of Nationalism*, London, Verso, 1991

Anderson, G., *Museum Mission Statements: Building a Distinctive Identity*, Washington DC, American Association of Museums, 2000

Anderson, M.L., 'A clear view: the case for museum transparency', *Museum*, vol.89, no.2, 2010, 48–53

Appadurai, A., (ed.). *The Social Life of Things: Commodities in Cultural Perspective*, Cambridge, Cambridge University Press, 1988

Appadurai, A., 'Introduction', in A. Appadurai (ed.), *The Social Life of Things: Commodities in Cultural Perspective*, Cambridge, Cambridge University Press, 1988

Applebaum, B., *Guide to Environmental Protection of Collections*, Madison, Sound View Press, 1991

Arnold, K., *Cabinets for the Curious*, Aldershot, Ashgate, 2006

Arts Council England and BOP Consulting, *Character Matters: Attitudes, Behaviours and Skills in the UK Museum Workforce* [online report], 2016, https://www.artscouncil.org.uk/sites/default/files/download-file/ACE_Museums_Workforce_ABS_BOP_Final_Report.pdf (accessed 1 September 2019)

Arts Council England, 'About Accreditation', *UK Museum Accreditation Scheme* [website], https://www.artscouncil.org.uk/accreditation-scheme/about-accreditation (accessed 18 July 2019)

Arts Council England, *Accreditation Guidance* [web resource], June 2014, https://www.artscouncil.org.uk/sites/default/files/download-file/FINAL_201406_GuidanceSection2_PrintFriendly.pdf (accessed 9 April 2019)

Ashby, H., McKenna, G., and Stiff, M., *SPECTRUM Knowledge Standards for Cultural Information Management*, Cambridge, MDA, 2001

Ashley-Smith, J., *Risk Assessment for Object Conservation*, London, Butterworth-Heinemann, 1999

Ashley-Smith, J., 'Risk Analysis', in C. Caple (ed.), *Preventive Conservation in Museums*, London, Routledge, 2012

Ashworth, G., *Heritage Planning: Conservation as the Management of Urban Change*, Groningen, Geo Pers, 1991

Askerud, P., and Clément, E., *Preventing the Illicit Traffic in Cultural Property: A Resource Handbook for the Implementation of the 1970 UNESCO Convention*, Paris, UNESCO, Division of Cultural Heritage, 1997

Australian Museum, *Learning Resources*, 'Writing Text and Labels', https://australianmuseum.net.au/learn/teachers/learning/writing-text-and-labels/, 2019 (accessed 7 June 2019)

Bachelor, R., 'Not Looking at Kettles', in S. Pearce (ed.), *Interpreting Objects and Collections*, London, Routledge, 1994

Backmann, K., *Conservation Concerns: A Guide for Collectors and Curators*, Washington DC, Smithsonian Institution Press, 1992

Baekeland, F., 'Psychological Aspects of Art Collecting', in S. Pearce (ed.), *Interpreting Objects and Collections*, London, Routledge, 1994

Barkan, E., and Bush. R., *Claiming the Stones / Naming the Bones: Cultural Property and the Negotiation of National and Ethnic Identity*, Los Angeles, Getty, 2003

Barringer, T., and Flynn, T. (eds), *Colonialism and the Object: Empire, Material Culture and the Museum*, London, Routledge, 1998

Baudrillard, J., 'The System of Collecting', in J. Elsner and R. Cardinal (eds), *The Cultures of Collecting*, London, Reaktion Books, 1994

BBC, 'London Museums Urged to Show More Hidden Artefacts', *BBC News* [website], 19 January 2011, https://www.bbc.co.uk/news/uk-england-london-12214145 (accessed 14 December 2018)

Bedford, L., *The Art of Museum Exhibitions: How Story and Imagination Create Aesthetic Experiences*, London, Routledge, 2016

Belcher, M., *Exhibitions in Museums*, Washington DC, Smithsonian Institution Press, 2000

Belk, R., 'Collectors and Collecting', in S. Pearce (ed.), *Interpreting Objects and Collections*, London, Routledge, 1994

Belk, R., Wallendorf, M., Sherry, J., and Holbrook, M., 'Collecting in a Consumer Culture', in *Highways and Buyways: Naturalistic Research from the Consumer Behavior Odyssey*, Provo, Association for Consumer Research, 1990

Bennes, C., 'Open the stores: conservation, collections and the museum of the future', *Apollo Magazine* [website], 13 June 2014, https://www.apollo-magazine.com/conservation-accessible-stores-museum-future/ (accessed 14 December 2018)

Bennett, T., *The Birth of the Museum: History, Theory, Politics*, London, Routledge, 1995

Bitgood, S., 'The ABCs of label design', in *Visitor Studies: Theory, Research and Practice*, vol.8, 1991, 115–29

Bitgood, S., 'Practical Guidelines for Developing Interpretive Labels', *Visitor Behaviour*, Fall, 1996, 4–15

Black, G., *The Engaging Museum: Developing Museums for Visitor Involvement*, London, Routledge, 2012

Blankenberg, N., 'Participatory Exhibitions', in B. Lord and M. Piacente (eds), *Manual of Museum Exhibitions*, Lanham, Rowman and Littlefield, 2nd edn, 2014

Blankenberg, N., 'Virtual Experiences', in B. Lord and M. Piacente (eds), *Manual of Museum Exhibitions*, 2nd edn, Lanham, Rowman and Littlefield, 2014

Bloom, B., *A Taxonomy for Learning, Teaching, and Assessing: A Revision of Bloom's Taxonomy of Educational Objectives*, New York, Longman, 2001

Bogle, E., *Museum Exhibition Planning and Design*, Lanham, AltaMira Press, 2013

Bond, N., and Falk, J.H., 'Who am I? And why am I here (and not there)? The role of identity in shaping tourist visit motivations', *International Journal of Tourism Research*, vol.15, no.15, 2012, 430–42,

Bourdieu, P., 'Symbolic power', *Critique of Anthropology*, vol.13, 1979, 77–85

Boyd, W., 'Museum accountability: laws, rules, ethics and accreditation', *Curator: The Museum Journal*, vol.34, no.3, 1991, 165–77

Boylan, P. (ed.), *Running a Museum: A Practical Handbook*, Paris, ICOM, 2004

Boylan, P., 'The Museum Profession', in S. Macdonald (ed.), *A Companion to Museum Studies*, Malden, Blackwell Publishing, 2006

Bradley, S., and Thickett, D., 'The Pollution Problem in Perspective', in C. Caple, *Preventive Conservation in Museums*, London, Routledge, 2012

British Museum, *A Guide to the Storage, Exhibition and Handling of Antiquities, Ethnographia and Pictorial Art*, London, British Museum Publications, 1990

Brodie, N., and Walker Tubb, K., *Illicit Antiquities: The Theft of Culture and the Extinction of Archaeology*, London, Routledge, 2012

Bruner, J., 'The act of discovery', *Harvard Educational Review*, vol.31, no.1, 1961, 21–32

Brüninghaus-Knubel, C., 'Museum Education in the Context of Museum Functions', in P. Boylan (ed.), *Running a Museum: A Practical Handbook*, Paris, ICOM, 2004

Buck, R., and Gilmore, J. (eds), *MRM5: Museum Registration Methods*, 5th edn, American Association of Museums Press, 2010

Bullock, L., 'Light as an Agent of Decay', in C. Caple (ed.), *Preventive Conservation in Museums*, London, Routledge, 2012

Burton, A., *The Development of Museums in Victorian Britain and the Contribution of the Society of Arts*, The William Shipley Group for RSA History, Occasional Paper, No.16, 2010

Cackett, S., 'Disaster Planning', in J.M.A. Thompson (ed.), *Manual of Curatorship*, 2nd edn, Oxford, Butterworth-Heinemann, 1992

Cameron, D., 'The museum, a temple or the forum', *Curator: The Museum Journal*, vol.14, no.1, 1971, 11–24

Cannon-Brookes, P., 'The Role of the Curator Scholar in Conservation', in S. Knell (ed.), *Care of Collections*, Abingdon, Routledge. 2005

Caple, C. (ed.), *Preventive Conservation in Museums*, London, Routledge, 2012

Caple, C., 'Conservation Skills: Preventive Conservation – Storage', in C. Caple (ed.), *Preventive Conservation in Museums*, London, Routledge, 2012

Cash, D., *Access to Museum Culture: The British Museum from 1753 to 1836*, British Museum Occasional Paper No.133,

2002, http://www.britishmuseum.org/research/publications/research_publications_series/2002/access_to_museum_culture.aspx (accessed 11 October 2018)

Cassar, M., *Environmental Management Guidelines for Museums and Galleries*, London, MGC and Routledge, 1995

Cassar, M., 'Environmental Management', in C. Caple (ed.), *Preventive Conservation in Museums*, London, Routledge, 2012

Cassman, V., Odegaard, N., and Powell, J. (eds), *Human Remains: Guide for Museums and Academic Institutions*, Lanham, AltaMira Press, 2008

Chatterjee, H., 'Staying essential: articulating the value of object based learning', *University Museums and Collections Journal*, vol.2, 2007, 121–5

Chatterjee, H., 'Object-based learning in higher education: the pedagogical power of museums', *University Museums and Collections Journal*, vol.3, 2010, 179–81

Clavir, M., 'Ethics and Theory in Preventive Conservation', in C. Caple (ed.), *Preventive Conservation in Museums*, London, Routledge, 2012

Collections Trust, 'Collections Management', *Collections Trust* [web resource], n.d., https://collectionstrust.org.uk/collections-management/ (accessed 13 February 2019)

Collections Trust, 'All Procedures', *Spectrum* [website], September 2017, https://collectionstrust.org.uk/spectrum/procedures/ (accessed 13 October 2019)

Collections Trust, 'Exit Forms', *Spectrum Related Resources* [web resource], 2017, https://collectionstrust.org.uk/resource/object-exit-forms/ (accessed 30 January 2019)

Collections Trust, 'Introduction to Spectrum 5.0', *Spectrum* [website], 2017, https://collectionstrust.org.uk/spectrum/spectrum-5/ (accessed 13 February 2019)

Collections Trust, 'Object Entry Forms', *Collections Trust* [web resource], 2017, https://collectionstrust.org.uk/resource/object-entry-forms/ (accessed 30 January 2019)

Collections Trust, 'Transfer of Title Forms', *Collections Development* [web resource], 2017, https://collectionstrust.org.uk/resource/transfer-of-title-forms/ (accessed 30 January 2019)

Collins, Z. (ed.), *Museums, Adults and the Humanities: A Guide for Educational Programming*, Washington DC, American Association of Museums, 1984

Corsane, G. (ed.), *Heritage, Museums and Galleries: An Introductory Reader*, London, Routledge, 2005

Cossons, N., 'Scholarship or Self-Indulgence?', in G. Kavanagh (ed.), *Museum Provision and Professionalism*, London, Routledge, 1994

Courtney, J. (ed.), *The Legal Guide for Museum Professionals*, New York, Rowman and Littlefield, 2015

Crossman, A., and Pinniger, D., *What's Eating Your Collection* [website], 2015, http://www.whatseatingyourcollection.com/ (accessed 8 May 2019)

Cuno, J., *Whose Culture? The Promise of Museums and the Debate Over Antiquities*, Princeton, Princeton University Press, 2012

Davies, P. (ed.), *Museums and the Disposals Debate*, Edinburgh, MuseumsEtc, 2011

Davis, J., *The MUSE Book*, Cambridge, President and Fellows of Harvard College/Harvard Project Zero, 1996

DCMS, 'Working Group on Human Remains, Report on Human Remains' [online report], 14 November 2003, https://webarchive.nationalarchives.gov.uk/+/http://www.culture.gov.uk/reference_library/publications/4553.aspx (accessed 9 September 2019)

DCMS, 'Guidance for the Care of Human Remains in Museums' [online report], 2005, https://www.britishmuseum.org/pdf/DCMS%20Guide.pdf (accessed 9 September 2019)

Dean, D., *Museum Exhibition: Theory and Practice*, Abingdon, Routledge, 1994

Department for Culture, Media and Sport, Cultural Property Unit, *Combating Illicit Trade: Due Diligence Guidelines for Museums, Libraries and Archives on Collecting and Borrowing Cultural Material*, London, DCMS, 2005

Desvallées, A., and Mairesse, F., *Key Concepts of Museology*, Paris, Armand Colin, 2010

Dewey, J., *Democracy and Education*, Milton Keynes, Simon and Brown, 2011 [1916]

Dexter Lord, G., Quiang, G., Laishun, A., and Jimenez, J. (eds), *Museum Development in China*, Lanham, Rowman and Littlefield, 2019

Dillon Wright, L., 'Curatorship and Content Development', in B. Lord and M. Piacente (eds), *Manual of Museum Exhibitions*, 2nd edn, Lanham, Rowman and Littlefield, 2014

Din, H., and Hecht, P., *The Digital Museum: A Think Guide*, Washington DC, American Association of Museums, 2007

Dodd, J., and Sandell. R., *Building Bridges: Guidance for Museums and Galleries on Developing New Audiences*, London, Museums & Galleries Commission, 1998

Dudley, D., and Wilkinson, I. (eds), *Museum Registration Methods*, Washington DC, American Association of Museums, 1989

Dudley, S., *Museum Materialities: Objects, Engagements, Interpretations*, London, Routledge, 2013

Duhs, R., 'Learning from university museums and collections in higher education: University College London (UCL)', *University Museums and Collections Journal*, vol.3, 183–6

Edson, G., 'Museum Management', in P. Boylan (ed.), *Running a Museum: A Practical Handbook*, Paris, ICOM, 2004

Ellis Burcaw, G., *Introduction to Museum Work*, 3rd edn, Lanham, AltaMira Press, 1983

Elsner, J., and Cardinal, R. (eds), *The Cultures of Collecting*, London, Reaktion Books, 1994

Eriksen, H., and Unger, I., *The Small Museums Cataloguing Manual*, Victoria, Museums Australia, 2009

Fahy, A. (ed.), *Collections Management*, Abingdon, Routledge, 1994

Fahy, A., 'Introduction', in A. Fahy (ed.), *Collections Management*, Abingdon, Routledge, 1994

Falk, J., *Identity and Museum Visitor Experience*, Walnut Creek, Left Coast Press, 2009

Falk, J., 'The use of time as a measure of visitor behaviour and exhibit effectiveness', *Roundtable Reports: The Journal of Museum Education*, vol.7, no.4, 1982, 10–13

Falk, J., and Dierking, L., *Learning from Museums: Visitor Experiences and the Making of Meaning*, Lanham, AltaMira Press, 2000

Falk, J., and Dierking, L., *The Museum Experience Revisited*, Walnut Creek, Left Coast Press, 2013

Ferguson, L.F., MacLulich, C., and Ravelli, L., *Meanings and Messages: Language Guidelines for Museum Exhibitions*, Sydney, Australian Museum, 1995

Fforde, C., Hubert J., and Turnbull, P. (eds), *The Dead and their Possessions: Repatriation in Principle, Policy and Practice*, London, Routledge, 2002

Fitz Gibbons, K. (ed.), *Who Owns the Past? Cultural Policy, Cultural Property, and the Law*, New Brunswick, Rutgers University Press, 2005

Fleming, D., Paine, C., and Rhodes, J. (eds), *Social History in Museums*, London, HMSO, 1993

Foley, M., and McPherson, G., 'Museums as leisure', *International Journal of Heritage Studies*, vol.6, no.2, 2000, 161–74

Fry, H., Ketteridge, S., and Marshall, S. (eds), *A Handbook for Teaching and Learning in Higher Education*, 3rd edn, London, Kogan Page, 2003

Gardner, H., *The Unschooled Mind*, New York, Basic Books, 1991

Gardner, H., *Intelligence Reframed: Multiple Intelligences for the 21st Century*, New York, Basic Books, 1999

Gardner, J., 'From Idiosyncratic to Integrated Strategic Planning for Collections', in C. McCarthy (ed.), *International Handbook of Museum Studies: Museum Practice*, London, Wiley-Blackwell, 2015

Gaventa, J., 'Power after Lukes: an vverview of theories of power since Lukes and their application to development', Brighton Participation Group, Institute of Development Studies [online article], 2003, https://www.powercube.net/wp-content/uploads/2009/11/power_after_lukes.pdf (accessed 13 October 2018)

Gell, A., *Art and Agency: An Anthropological Theory*, Oxford, Clarendon Press, 1998

George, A., *The Curator's Handbook*, London, Thames & Hudson, 2015

Getty Conservation Institute, 'Preventative Conservation', in S. Knell (ed.), *Care of Collections*, Abingdon, Routledge, 2005

Glaser, J., and Zenetou, A., *Museums: A Place to Work*, London, Routledge, 1996

Gosden, C., and Marshall, Y., 'The cultural biography of objects', *World Archaeology*, vol.31, no.2, 1999, 169–78

Graham, G., Ashworth, G., and Tunbridge, J., 'The Uses and Abuses of Heritage', in G. Corsane (ed.), *Heritage, Museums and Galleries: An Introductory Reader*, London, Routledge, 2005

Greenfield, J., *The Return of Cultural Treasures*, 3rd edn, New York, Cambridge University Press, 2007

Griffith, E., 'Liability and Risk Management for Museums', in A. Fahy (ed.), *Collections Management*, London, Routledge, 1994

Griswold, W., *Cultures and Societies in a Changing World*, 4th edn, Thousand Oaks, Sage Publications, 2013

Gruber, M., Gelma, B., and Ranganath, C., 'States of curiosity modulate hippocampus-dependent learning via the dopaminergic circuit', *Neuron*, vol.84, no.2, 2014, 486–96

Gurian, E., 'A blurring of the boundaries', *Curator: The Museum Journal*, vol.38, no.1, 1995, 31–7

Gwinn, N., and Wellheiser, J. (eds), *Preparing for the Worst, Planning for the Best: Protecting our Cultural Heritage from Disaster*, München, Saur, 2005

Hall, M., *On Display*, 2nd edn, London, Lund Humphries, 1992

Hansen, B., *Great Exhibits! An Exhibit Planning and Construction Handbook for Small Museums*, Lanham, Rowman and Littlefield, 2017

Harrison, J., 'Ideas of Museums in the 1990s', in G. Gorsane (ed.), *Heritage, Museums and Galleries: An Introductory Reader*, London, Routledge, 2004

Harrison, R., *Heritage: Critical Approaches*, London, Routledge, 2012

Hein, G., *Learning in the Museum*, London, Routledge, 1998

Herreman, Y., 'Display, Exhibits and Exhibitions', in P. Boylan (ed.), *Running a Museum: A Practical Handbook*, Paris, ICOM, 2004

Hilberry, J., and Weinberg, S., 'Museum Collections Storage', in S. Knell (ed.), *Care of Collections*, Abingdon, Routledge, 2005

Hill, K., *Culture and Class in English Public Museums, 1850–1914*, Aldershot, Ashgate, 2005

Hillhouse, S., *Collections Management: A Practical Guide*, Cambridge, Collections Trust, 2009

Hodder, I., 'The Contextual Analysis of Symbolic Meanings', in S. Pearce (ed.), *Interpreting Objects and Collections*, London, Routledge, 1994

Hodder, I., 'The "Social" in Archaeological Theory: An Historical and Contemporary Perspective', in L. Meskell and R. Pruecel (eds), *A Companion to Social Archaeology*, Malden, Blackwell, 2003

Holm, S.A., *Guidelines for Constructing a Museum Object Name Thesaurus*, Cambridge, MDA, 1993

Holm, S.A., *Facts and Artefacts. How to Document a Museum Collection*, Cambridge, MDA, 1998

Hood, M., 'Staying away – why people choose not to visit museums', *Museum News*, vol.61, no.4, 1983, 50–57

Hood, M., 'Audience Research Tells Us Why Visitors Come to Museums – and Why they Don't', in C. Scott (ed.), *Evaluation and Visitor Research in Museums: Towards 2000*. Sydney, Powerhouse Publishing, 1996

Hooper-Greenhill, E., *Learning and Teaching with Objects: A Practical Skills Based Approach*, Leicester, Department of Museum Studies, University of Leicester, 1988

Hooper-Greenhill, E., *Museums and Interpretive Communities*, Sydney, Australian Museum Audience Research Centre, 1999

Hooper-Greenhill, E., *Museums and the Interpretation of Visual Culture*, London, Routledge, 2008

Hooper-Greenhill, E., *Museums and their Visitors*, London, Routledge, 2012

Hooper-Greenhill, E., *Museums and Education: Purpose, Pedagogy, Performance*, London, Routledge, 2010

Hooper-Greenhill, E. (ed.), *The Educational Role of the Museum*, 2nd edn, New York, Routledge, 1999

Hooper-Greenhill, E., 'Studying Visitors', in S. Macdonald (ed.), *A Companion to Museum Studies*, Malden, Blackwell, 2006

Hooper-Greenhill, E., 'The Characteristics and Significance of Learning in Museums', in E. Hooper-Greenhill, *Museums and Education: Purpose, Pedagogy, Performance*, London, Routledge, 2010

Hoskins, J., *Biographical Objects: How Things Tell the Stories of Peoples' Lives*, New York, Routledge, 1998

Hoskins, J., 'Agency, Biography, and Objects', in C. Tilley, et al. (eds), *Handbook of Material Culture*, London, Sage Publications, 2017

Howie, F. (ed.), *Safety in Museums and Galleries*, London, Butterworth-Heinemann, 1987

Hudson, K., *Museums for the 1980s: A Survey of World Trends*, Paris, UNESCO/Macmillan, 1977

Hunter, J., 'Museum Disaster Preparedness and Planning', in C. Caple (ed.), *Preventive Conservation in Museums*. London, Routledge, 2012

ICOM, 'About ICOM', *ICOM* [website], n.d., http://umac.icom.museum/membership/about-icom/ (accessed 10 October 2018)

ICOM, 'ICOM Code of Ethics for Museums', *ICOM* [website], 2004, https://icom.museum/wp-content/uploads/2018/07/ICOM-code-En-web.pdf (accessed 12 December 2018)

ICOM, 'Missions and Objectives', *ICOM* [website], 2016, https://icom.museum/en/about-us/missions-and-objectives/ (accessed 10 October 2018)

ICOM, 'Museum Definition', *ICOM* [website], 2018, https://icom.museum/en/activities/standards-guidelines/museum-definition/ (accessed 11 October 2018)

International Council of Museums Conference New York (City) and International Council of Museums, *Papers from the Seventh General Conference of ICOM*, Metropolitan Museum, New York, 1965

Janes, R., *Museums in a Troubled World: Renewal, Irrelevance or Collapse?*, London, Routledge, 2012

Jenkins, H., Clinton, K., Purushotma, R., Robison, A.J., and Weigel, M., 'Confronting the Challenge of Participatory Culture: Media Education for the 21st Century', *MacArthur* [digital version], 2009, https://www.macfound.org/media/article_pdfs/JENKINS_WHITE_PAPER.PDF (accessed 29 August 2019)

Jenkins, I., *Disaster Planning and Preparedness*, London, British Library, 1987

Jirásek, P., 'Museum Security, including Disaster Preparedness', in P. Boylan (ed.), *Running a Museum: A Practical Handbook*, Paris, ICOM, 2004

Johnson, P., 'Introduction to Collection Management and Development', in P. Johnson, *Fundamentals of Collection Development*, 2nd edn, Chicago, The American Library Association, 2018

Jones, B., 'Experiencing Loss', in S. Knell (ed.), *Care of Collections*, Abingdon, Routledge, 2005

Karp, I., Kreamer, C., and Lavine, S. (eds), *Museums and Communities: The Politics of Public Culture*, Washington DC, Smithsonian Institution Press, 1992

Kassim, S., 'The museum will not be decolonised', *Media Diversified* [article], 2017, https://mediadiversified.

org/2017/11/15/the-museum-will-not-be-decolonised/ (accessed 12 September 2019)

Keene, S., *Managing Conservation in Museums*, Oxford, Butterworth-Heinemann, 1996

Keene, S., Stevenson, A., and Monti, F., 'Collections for people: museums' stored collections as a public resource', *UCL Institute of Archaeology* [online report], 2008, http://discovery.ucl.ac.uk/13886/1/13886.pdf (accessed 12 August 2019). 'Too much stuff: disposal from museums', National Museum Directors' Conference [web resource], 2003, https://www.nationalmuseums.org.uk/media/documents/publications/too_much_stuff.pdf (accessed 11 December 2018)

Klobe, T., *Exhibitions: Concept, Planning and Design*, Chicago, University of Chicago Press, 2013

Knappett, C., 'Animacy, Agency, and Personhood', in *Thinking through Material Culture: An Interdisciplinary Perspective*, Philadelphia, University of Pennsylvania Press, 2005

Knell, S. (ed.), *Care of Collections*, Abingdon, Routledge, 2005

Knell, S. (ed.), *Museums and the Future of Collecting*, 2nd edn, Abingdon, Routledge, 2016

Knell, S., 'The shape of things to come: museums in the technological landscape', *Museum and Society*, vol.1, no.3, 2003

Knell, S., 'Introduction: The Context of Collections Care', in S. Knell (ed.), *Care of Collections*, Abingdon, Routledge. 2005

Kolb, D., *Experiential Learning Experience as the Source of Learning and Development*, Englewood Cliffs, Prentice Hall, 2003 [1984]

Kopytoff, I., 'The Cultural Biography of Things: Commoditization as Process', in A. Appadurai (ed.), *The Social Life of Things: Commodities in Cultural Perspective*, Cambridge, Cambridge University Press, 1986

Kreps, C., 'Changing the Rules of the Road: Postcolonialism and the New Ethics of Museum Anthropology', in J. Marstine (ed.), *The Routledge Companion to Museum Ethics: Redefining Ethics for the Twenty-First-Century Museum*, New York, Routledge, 2011

Kreps, C., 'Indigenous Curation, Museums, and Intangible Cultural Heritage', in L. Smith and N. Akagawa (eds), *Intangible Heritage: The Practices and Politics of Safeguarding*, 2nd edn, Abingdon, Routledge, 2018

Kuruvilla, H., *A Legal Dictionary for Museums*, Lanham, Rowman and Littlefield, 2016

Ladkin, N., 'Collections Management', in P. Boylan (ed.), *Running a Museum: A Practical Handbook*, Paris, ICOM, 2004

Lane, R., *Jean Baudrillard*, New York, Routledge, 2000

Lang, C., Reeve, J., and Woollard, V. (eds), *The Responsive Museum: Working with Audiences in the Twenty-First Century*, London, Routledge, 2016

Lave, J., and Wenger, E., *Situated Learning: Legitimate Peripheral Participation*, Cambridge, Cambridge University Press, 1991

León, S., *Uppity Women of Ancient Times*, Berkeley, Conari Press, 1995

Lewis, G., 'Attitudes to Disposal from Museum Collections', in A. Fahy (ed.), *Collections Management*, Abingdon, Routledge, 1994

Lewis, G., 'Deaccessioning and the ICOM Code of Ethics', *ICOM News*, vol.56, no.1, 2003

Lewis, G., 'The Role of Museums and the Professional Code of Ethics', in P. Boylan (ed.), *Running a Museum: A Practical Handbook*, Paris, ICOM, 2004

Linnie, M., 'Pest Control in Museums: The Use of Chemicals and Associated Health Problems', in S. Knell (ed.), *Care of Collections*, Abingdon, Routledge, 2005

Liston, D. (ed.), *Museum Security and Protection: A Handbook for Cultural Heritage Institutions*, London, Routledge, 1993

Lloyd, H., and Lithgow, K., 'Physical Agents of Deterioration: Dust and Dirt', in C. Caple (ed.), *Preventive Conservation in Museums*, London, Routledge, 2012

Logan, W., and Reeves K. (eds), *Places of Pain and Shame: Dealing with 'Difficult' Heritage*, London, Routledge, 2009

Longair, S., and McAleer, J. (eds), *Curating Empire: Museums and the British Imperial Experience*, Manchester, Manchester University Press, 2012

Lord, B., 'The Purpose of Museum Exhibitions', in B. Lord and M. Piacente (eds), *Manual of Museum Exhibitions*, 2nd edn, Lanham, Rowman and Littlefield, 2014

Lord, B., 'Where Do Exhibition Ideas Come From?', in B. Lord and M. Piacente (eds), *Manual of Museum Exhibitions*, 2nd edn, Lanham, Rowman and Littlefield, 2014

Lord, B., and Piacente, M. (eds), *Manual of Museum Exhibitions*, Lanham, Rowman and Littlefield, 2nd edn, 2014

Lord, G., 'Measuring Success', in B. Lord and M. Piacente, *Manual of Museum Exhibitions*, 2nd edn, Lanham, Rowman and Littlefield, 2014

Lorde, A, 'The Master's Tools Will Never Dismantle the Master's House', in A. Lorde, *Sister Outsider: Essays and Speeches*, Trumansburg, Crossing Press, 2007

B. Lord, G. Dexter Lord and L. Martin, *The Manual of Museum Planning: Sustainable Space, Facilities, and Operation*, 3rd edn, Lanham, AltaMira Press, 2012

McCarthy, C. (ed.), *International Handbook of Museum Studies: Museum Practice*, London, Wiley-Blackwell, 2015

MacDermott J., (ed.), *The Philosophy of John Dewey*, 2 vols, Chicago, University of Chicago Press, 1973

Macdonald, S. (ed.), *A Companion to Museum Studies*, Malden, Blackwell Publishing, 2006

Macdonald, S., 'Collecting Practices', in S. Macdonald (ed.), *A Companion to Museum Studies*, Malden, Blackwell Publishing, 2006

McGillivray, W., 'Museum research: axiom or oxymoron', *Muse*, vol.9, no.2, 1991, 62–6

MacGregor, N., in Culture, Media and Sport Committee, *Oral Evidence: Countries of Culture*, HC 864, Questions 127–85 [online], 2016. available at: http://data.parliament.uk/writtenevidence/committeeevidence.svc/evidencedocument/culture-media-and-sport-committee/countries-of-culture/oral/32902.html (accessed 10 May 2018)

MacKenzie, J., *Museums and Empire: Natural History, Human Cultures and Colonial Identities*, Manchester, Manchester University Press, 2009

McLean, K., *Planning for People in Exhibitions*, Washington DC, Association of Science-Technology Centers, 1993

McManus, P., 'Oh, yes, they do: how museum visitors read labels and interact with exhibit texts', *Curator: The Museum Journal*, vol.32, no.3, 1989, 174–89

Malaro, M., 'Collection Management Policies', in A. Fahy (ed.), *Collections Management*, Abingdon, Routledge, 1994

Malaro, M., and DeAngelis, I., *A Legal Primer on Managing Museum Collections*, 3rd edn, Washington DC, Smithsonian Books, 2012

Marstine, J. (ed.), *The Routledge Companion to Museum Ethics: Redefining Ethics for the Twenty-First-Century Museum*, New York, Routledge, 2011

Marty, P., and Burton Jones, K., *Museum Informatics: People, Information, and Technology in Museums*, New York, Routledge, 2009

Mason, R., 'Museums, Galleries and Heritage', in G. Corsane (ed.), *Heritage, Museums and Galleries: An Introductory Reader*, London, Routledge, 2010

Matassa, F., *Organising Exhibitions: A Handbook for Museums, Libraries and Archives*, London, Facet Publishing, 2014

Mayer, C., 'The contemporary curator – endangered species or brave new profession', *Muse*, Summer/Autumn, 1991, 34–8

Merriman, N., 'Museum collections and sustainability', *Cultural Trends*, vol.17, no.1, 2008, 3–21, DOI: 10.1080/09548960801920278

Merritt, E. (ed.), *Covering Your Assets: Facilities and Risk Management in Museums*, American Association of Museums, 2005

Merryman, J., *Imperialism, Art, and Restitution*, New York, Cambridge University Press, 2006

Mervin, R., and Mecklenburg, M.F., *Art in Transit: Handbook for Packing and Transporting Paintings*, Washington DC, National Gallery of Art, 1991

Message, K., *New Museums and the Making of Culture*, Oxford, Berg, 2006

Michalski, S., 'Care and Preservation of Collections', in P. Boylan (ed.), *Running a Museum: A Practical Handbook*, Paris, ICOM, 2004

Michalski, S., 'Relative Humidity and Temperature Guidelines', in C. Caple (ed.), *Preventive Conservation in Museums*, London, Routledge, 2012

Miles, G., 'Object Handling', in C. Caple (ed.), *Preventive Conservation in Museums*, London, Routledge, 2012

Miller, B., and McKune, A., 'In a generous spirit: museums as donees: standards, best practice and ethical and legal responsibilities', *Museum*, vol.90, no.4, 2011, 50–52

Miller, E., *That Noble Cabinet: A History of the British Museum*, Athens, Ohio University Press, 1974

Moffat, H., and Woollard, V. (eds), *Museum and Gallery Education: A Manual of Good Practice*, Walnut Creek, AltaMira Press, 2004

Molineux, K., 'Permanent Collection Displays', in B. Lord and M. Piacente (eds), *Manual of Museum Exhibitions*, 2nd edn, Lanham, Rowman and Littlefield, 2014

Moran, J., 'Curiosity is an inextinguishable creative spark', *Times Higher Education* [online article], 2017, https://www.timeshighereducation.com/comment/curiosity-is-an-inextinguishable-creative-spark (accessed 26 August 2019)

Moussouri, T., and Roussos, G., 'Examining the effect of visitor motivation on visit strategies using mobile computer technologies', *Visitor Studies*, vol.16, no.1, 2013, 21–38

Museums Association, 'Acquisition: Guidance on the Ethics and Practicalities of Acquisition', *Ethical Guidelines: Advice from the Museums Association Ethics Committee* [web resource], 2004, https://www.museumsassociation.org/download?id=11114 (accessed 18 July 2019)

Museums Association, *Public Perceptions of – and Attitudes to – the Purposes of Museums in Society* [online report], 2013, https://www.museumsassociation.org/download?id=954916 (accessed 22 August 2019)

Museums Association, 'Code of Ethics for Museums', *Museums Association* [website] 2015, https://www.

museumsassociation.org/download?id=1155827 (accessed 7 January 2019)

National Parks Service, 'How To Select Gloves: An Overview For Collections Staff', *National Parks Service, Conserve O Gram*, September 2010, No.1/12, https://www.nps.gov/museum/publications/conserveogram/01-12.pdf (accessed 9 April 2019)

National Trust, *The National Trust Manual of Housekeeping*, rev. edn, London, National Trust, 2011

Nauert, P., and Black, C., *Fine Arts Insurance: A Handbook for Art Museums*, Washington DC, Association of Art Museum Directors, 1979

Negri, M. (ed.), *New Museums in Europe 1977–1983*, Milan, Mazzotta, 1984

Newman, A., 'Understanding the Social Impact of Museums, Galleries and Heritage through the Concept of Capital', in G. Corsane (ed.), *Heritage, Museums and Galleries: An Introductory Reader*, London, Routledge, 2005

Nicholson, E., and Williams, E., 'Developing a working definition for the museum collection', *Inside Line*, Fall 2002, 1–4

Nicks, J., 'Collections Management', in B. Lord, G. Dexter Lord and L. Martin (eds), *The Manual of Museum Planning: Sustainable Space, Facilities and Operations*, 3rd edn, Lanham, AltaMira Press, 2012

Norbert, S., and Banks, P., 'Indoor Air Pollution: Effects on Cultural and Historic Materials', in S. Knell (ed.), *Care of Collections*, Abingdon, Routledge, 2005

O'Keefe, P., *Commentary on the UNESCO 1970 Convention on Illicit Traffic*, Leicester, Institute of Art and Law, 2002

O'Reilly, P., and Lord, A., *Basic Condition Reporting: A Handbook*, New York, South East Registrars' Association, 1988

Orna, E., *Build Yourself a Thesaurus: A Step by Step Guide*, Norwich, Running Angel, 1983

Ortony, A., Norman, D., and Revelle, W., 'Affect and Proto-affect in Effective Functioning', in J. Fellous, and M. Arbib (eds), *Who Needs Emotions? The Brain Meets the Robot*, Oxford, Oxford University Press, 2005

Ovenel, R., *The Ashmolean Museum, 1683–1894*, Oxford, Clarendon Press, 1986

Paddon, H., *Redisplaying Museum Collections: Contemporary Display and Interpretation in British Museums*, Abingdon, Routledge, 2016

Pavlov, I., *Lectures on Conditioned Reflexes: Twenty-Five Years of Objective Study of the High Nervous Activity (Behavior) of Animals*, translated by W. Horsley Gantt. New York, International, 1928

Pearce, S. (ed.), *Interpreting Objects and Collections*, London, Routledge, 1994

Pearce, S., *On Collecting: An Investigation into Collecting in the European Tradition*, London, Routledge, 1995

Pearce, S., 'Collecting Reconsidered', in S. Pearce (ed.), *Interpreting Objects and Collections*, London, Routledge, 1994

Pearce, S., 'Objects as Meaning', in S. Pearce (ed.), *Interpreting Objects and Collections*, London, Routledge, 1994

Pearce, S., 'The Urge to Collect', in S. Pearce (ed.), *Interpreting Objects and Collections*, London, Routledge, 1994

Pearce, S., 'Thinking About Things', in S. Pearce (ed.), *Interpreting Objects and Collections*, London, Routledge, 1994

Pekarik, A., Doering, Z., and Karns, D., 'Exploring satisfying experiences in museums', *Curator: The Museum Journal*, vol.42, no.2, 1999, 152–73

Phillips, R., 'The accumulator', *Archives of General Psychiatry*, vol.6, 1962, 474–7

Piacente, M., 'Interpretive Planning', in B. Lord and M. Piacente (eds), *Manual of Museum Exhibitions*, 2nd edn, Lanham, Rowman and Littlefield, 2014

Piaget, J., *Origins of Intelligence in the Child*, London, Routledge & Kegan Paul, 1936

Piaget, J., *The Psychology of Intelligence*, London, Routledge and Kegan Paul, 1950

Pinniger, D., *Pest Management – A Practical Guide*, London, Collections Trust, 2008

Pinniger, D., *Integrated Pest Management in Cultural Heritage*, London, Archetype Publications, 2015

Pinniger, D., *Pests in Houses Great and Small*, London, English Heritage, 2018

Pitman, B., 'Muses, museums, and memories', *Daedalus*, vol.128, no.3, 1999, 1–31

Powell, B., and Richard, M., *Collection Care: An Illustrated Handbook for the Care and Handling of Cultural Objects*, Lanham, Rowman & Littlefield, 2016

Prentice, R., 'Heritage: A Key Sector in the "New" Tourism', in G. Corsane (ed.), *Heritage, Museums and Galleries: An Introductory Reader*, London, Routledge, 2005

Prott, L., 'Illicit Traffic', in P. Boylan (ed.), *Running a Museum: A Practical Handbook*, Paris, ICOM, 2004

Punt, B., Stern, S., and Ratcliffe, S., *Doing It Right: A Workbook for Improving Exhibit Labels*, Brooklyn, The Museum, 1989

Resource: The Council for Museums, Archives and Libraries, *Security in Museums, Archives and Libraries: A Practical Guide*, London, Resource, 2003

Roberts, A., *Planning the Documentation of Museum Collections*, Cambridge, MDA, 1985

Roberts, A., 'Inventories and Documentation', in P. Boylan (ed.), *Running a Museum: A Practical Handbook*, Paris, ICOM, 2004

Roppola, T., *Designing for the Museum Visitor Experience*, New York, Routledge, 2014

Ross, M., 'Interpreting the new museology', *Museum and Society*, vol.2, no.2, 2004, 84–103

Rydera, S., and Mendez, A., *Designing and Planning Space with IPM in Mind – The Darwin Centre Phase Two*, Presented at 11th International Working Conference on Stored Product Protection, 2014

Samson, D., 'Reading Strategies Used by Exhibition Visitors', in A. Blais (ed.), *Text in the Exhibition Medium*, Québec City, Musée de la civilisation, 1995

Sandell, R., *Museums, Prejudice and the Reframing of Difference*, London, Routledge, 2007

Satwicz, T., and Morrissey, K., 'Public Curation: From Trend to Research-based Practice', in B. Adair, B. Filene and L. Koloski (eds), *Letting Go? Sharing Historical Authority in a User-Generated World*, Philadelphia, Pew Center for Arts and Heritage, 2011

Schlereth, T., 'Contemporary collecting for future recollecting', *The Museum Studies Journal*, vol.1, no.3, 1984, 23–30

Schulz, E., 'Notes on the History of Collecting and of Museums', in S. Pearce (ed.), *Interpreting Objects and Collections*. London, Routledge, 1994

Scott, C. (ed.), *Evaluation and Visitor Research in Museums: Towards 2000*, Sydney, Powerhouse Publishing, 1996

Screven, C., 'Motivating visitors to read labels', *ILVS Review: A Journal of Visitor Behaviour*, vol.2, no.2, 1992, 183–211

Serrell, B., *Exhibit Labels: An Interpretive Approach*, Walnut Creek, AltaMira Press, 1996

Serrell, B., 'Paying attention: the duration and allocation of visitors' time in museum exhibitions', *Curator: The Museum Journal*, vol.40, no.2, 1997, 108–25

Simmons, J., *Things Great and Small: Collections Management Policies*, 2nd edn, Lanham, Rowman and Littlefield, 2018

Simmons, J., 'Collections Care and Management: History, Theory, and Practice', in C. McCarthy (ed.), *International Handbook of Museum Studies: Museum Practice*, London, Wiley-Blackwell, 2015

Simon, N., *The Participatory Museum* [online book], 2010, http://www.participatorymuseum.org/read/ (accessed 3 June 2019)

Sjoberg, C., 'Addressing Learning Styles in the Interpretive Plan', in B. Lord and M. Piacente (eds), *Manual of Museum Exhibitions*, 2nd edn, Lanham, Rowman and Littlefield, 2014

Skinner, B., *Science and Human Behavior*, New York, Macmillan, 1953

Smith, L., 'Deaccessioning', *Registrars' Quarterly*, Winter, 1992, 1–2

Sola, T., 'Redefining Collecting', in S. Knell (ed.), *Museums and the Future of Collecting*, 2nd edn, Abingdon, Routledge, 2016

South Western Federation of Museums and Galleries, 'Developing a Collections Management Framework', *Collections Trust* [website], 2015, https://collectionstrust.org.uk/resource/developing-a-collections-management-framework/ (accessed 20 February 2019)

Stainton, C., 'Voice and Images: Making Connections Between Identity and Art', in G. Leinhardt, K. Crowley and K. Knutson (eds), *Learning Conversations in Museums*, Mahwah, Erlbaum Associates, 2002

Stam, D., 'The Informed Muse', in G. Corsane (ed.), *Heritage, Museums and Galleries: An Introductory Reader*, London, Routledge, 2010

Staniforth, S., 'Light and Environmental Control and Measurement in National Trust Houses', in S. Knell (ed.), *Care of Collections*, Abingdon, Routledge, 2005

Stenger, M., 'Why curiosity enhances learning', *Edutopia* [online article], 2014, https://www.edutopia.org/blog/why-curiosity-enhances-learning-marianne-stenger (accessed 26 August 2019)

Stolow, N., *Conservation and Exhibitions: Packing, Transport, Storage and Environmental Considerations*, London, Butterworth-Heinemann, 1987

Stone, S., 'Documenting Collections', in J. Thompson (ed.), *Manual of Curatorship*, 2nd edn, Oxford, Butterworth-Heinemann, 1992

Strohmaier, R., Sprung, G., Nischelwitze, A., and Schadenbauer, S., 'Using visitor-flow visualization to improve visitor experience in museums and exhibitions', MW2015: *Museums and the Web 2015* [website], 15 January 2015, https://mw2015.museumsandtheweb.com/paper/enhancing-visitor-experience-and-fostering-museum-popularity-through-deep-insights-in-the-placement-of-exhibits-by-new-techniques-in-visitor-flow-visualization-in-space-and-time/ (accessed 12 August 2019)

Strong, R., 'Scholar or salesman? The curator of the future', *Muse*, vol.6, no.2, 1988, 16–20

Summers, J., *Creating Exhibits That Engage*, Lanham, Rowman and Littlefield, 2018

Tallom, L., and Walker, K. (eds), *Digital Technologies and the Museum Experience*, Lanham, AltaMira Press, 2008

Tang, Y., and Mayrand, Y., 'Design', in B. Lord and M. Piacente (eds), *Manual of Museum Exhibitions*, 2nd edn, Lanham, Rowman and Littlefield, 2014

Teather, J., *Professional Directions for Museum Work in Canada*, Ottawa, Canadian Museums Association, 1978

The Government of the United Kingdom, 'Human Tissue Act 2004', *Guidance for Professionals* [website], https://www.hta.gov.uk/policies/human-tissue-act-2004 (accessed 9 September 2019)

The J. Paul Getty Museum, *Complete Guide*, 'Complete guide to adult audience interpretive materials: gallery texts and graphics', https://www.getty.edu/education/museum_educators/downloads/aaim_completeguide.pdf, 2011 (accessed 7 June 2019)

The Museum Pests Working Group (MP-WG), 'Identification', *Museum Pests* [website], 2019, https://museumpests.net/identification/ (accessed 8 May 2019)

The Museum Pests Working Group (MP-WG), 'Monitoring', *Museum Pests* [website], 2019, https://museumpests.net/monitoring-introduction/ (accessed 8 May 2019)

The Museum Pests Working Group (MP-WG), 'Solutions', *Museum Pests* [website], 2019, https://museumpests.net/solutions/ (accessed 8 May 2019)

Thomas, D. (ed.), *Museums in Postcolonial Europe*, London, Routledge, 2010

Thomas, N., *Entangled Objects: Exchange, Material Culture, and Colonialism in the Pacific*, Cambridge, Harvard University Press, 1991

Thompson, J. (ed.), *Manual of Curatorship*, 2nd edn, Oxford, Butterworth-Heinemann, 1992

Thornes, R., *Protecting Cultural Objects Through International Documentation Standards*, Santa Monica, The Getty Art History Information Programme, 1995

Tilden, F., *Interpreting Our Heritage*, 4th edn, Chapel Hill, University of North Carolina Press, 2008

Tilley, C., 'Ethnography and Material Culture', in P. Atkinson et al. (eds), *Handbook of Ethnography*, London, Sage Publications, 2001

Tilley, C., Keane, W., Küchler, S., Rowlands, M., and Spyer, P. (eds), *Handbook of Material Culture*, London, Sage Publications, 2006

Turner, B.S., *Status*, Milton Keynes, Open University Press, 1988

UNESCO, *Convention on the Means of Prohibiting and Preventing the Illicit Import, Export and Transfer of Ownership of Cultural Property*, 1970, http://www.unesco.org/new/en/culture/themes/illicit-trafficking-of-cultural-property/1970-convention/ (accessed 12 September 2019)

UNIDROIT, *UNIDROIT Convention on Stolen or Illegally Exported Cultural Objects*, 1995, https://www.unidroit.org/instruments/cultural-property/1995-convention (accessed 12 September 2019)

V&A, *Gallery Text at the V&A: A Ten Point Guide* [online resource], 2009, http://media.vam.ac.uk/media/documents/legacy_documents/file_upload/10808_file.pdf (accessed 7 June 2019)

Van Horn, D., Culligan, H., and Midgett, C., *Basic Condition Reporting*, 4th edn, Southeastern Registrars' Association, Lanham, Rowman and Littlefield, 2015

Vawda, S., 'Museums and the epistemology of injustice: from colonialism to decoloniality', *Museum International*, vol.71, no.1, 2019, 72–9

Veblen, T., *The Theory of the Leisure Class: An Economic Study in the Evolution of Institutions*, London, Allen & Unwin, 1924

Velarde, G., *Designing Exhibitions: Museums, Heritage, Trade and World Fairs*, Aldershot, Ashgate, 2001

Vergo, P. (ed.), *The New Museology*, London, Reaktion Books, 1989

Vrdoljak, A., *International Law, Museums and the Return of Cultural Objects*, New York, Cambridge University Press, 2006

Vreeland, R., 'Donation process and procedure outline', *Museum*, vol.90, no.4, 2011, 2–53

Vygotsky, L., *Mind in Society: The Development of Higher Psychological Processes*, Cambridge, Harvard University Press, 1978 [1930–34]

Wacquant, L., 'Habitus', in J. Becket and Z. Milan (eds), *International Encyclopaedia of Economic Sociology*, London, Routledge, 2005

Walhimer, M., *Museums 101*, Lanham, Rowman and Littlefield, 2015

Waller, R., *A Risk Model for Collection Preservation*, International Council of Museums, Committee for Conservation, Preprints of the 13th Triennial Meeting, Rio de Janeiro, 2002

Ware, M., *Museum Collecting Policies and Loan Agreements*, AIM Guideline 14, Association of Independent Museums, 1988

Watson, J., 'Psychology as the behaviorist views it', *Psychological Review*, vol.20, no.2, 1913, 158–77

Weil, S., *Rethinking the Museum and Other Meditations*, Washington DC, Smithsonian Institution Press, 1990

Weil, S., *Making Museums Matter*, Washington DC, Smithsonian Institution Press, 2002

Weil, S. (ed.), 'The Multiple Crises in our Museums', in Weil, S. (ed.), *Beauty and the Beasts: On Museums, Art, the Law, and the Market*, Washington DC, Smithsonian Institute, 1990

Weil, S., *A Deaccession Reader*, Washington DC, American Association of Museums, 1997

Weil, S. (ed.), 'Deaccession practices in American museums', *Museum News*, vol.65, no.3, 1987, 5–15

Weil, S., 'From being about something to being for somebody: the ongoing transformation of the American museum', *Daedalus*, vol.128, no.3, 1999, 229–58

Wilkening, S., and Chung, J., *Life Stages of the Museum Visitor: Building Engagement Over a Lifetime*, Washington DC, AAM Press, 2009

Wilson, P., 'The Clore Gallery for the Turner Collections at the Tate Gallery: Lighting Strategy and Practice', in S. Knell (ed.), *Care of Collections*, Abingdon, Routledge, 2005

Wintle, C., 'Decolonising the museum: the case of the Imperial and Commonwealth Institutes', *Museum and Society*, vol.1, no.2, 2013, 185–201

Woollard, V., 'Caring for the Visitor', in P. Boylan (ed.), *Running a Museum: A Practical Handbook*, Paris, ICOM, 2004

Woolley, L., *Excavations at Ur – A Record of Twelve Years' Work by Sir Leonard Woolley*, London, Ernest Benn Limited, 1955

Woolley, L., *Ur "of the Chaldees": The Final Account. Excavations at Ur*, New York, Herbert Press, 1982

Wylie, E., and Brophy, S., *The Green Museum: A Primer on Environmental Practice*, Lanham, AltaMira Press, 2008

Yerkovich, S., *A Practical Guide to Museum Ethics*, Lanham, Rowman and Littlefield, 2016

Young, J., and Buck, C. (eds), *The Ethics of Cultural Appropriation*, New York, Wiley-Blackwell, 2009

Index